PHILLIP WEARNE is a freelance journalist who has lived and worked in Mexico and Central America between 1981 and 1983 and has since made frequent visits to the region. He is founder and Director of *Latin American Monitor*, a news and information service based in London. He would like to pay special thanks to the development workers, clergy and indigenous people in Guatemala who helped to compile this report despite considerable personal risks.

Professor PETER CALVERT is Professor of Comparative and International Politics at the University of Southampton, specializing in the politics of the USA and Latin America. Among his publications are *Guatemala, A Nation in Turmoil* (Westview Press, 1985) and (Ed.) *The Central American Security System, North-South or East-West?* (Cambridge University Press, 1988).

The Maya of Guatemala

PHILLIP WEARNE with Prof. PETER C.

GW00702248

British Library Cataloguing in Publication Data

A CIP catalogue record for this book is available from the British Library.

ISBN No 0 946690 69 3

First published December 1989

The report that follows has been commissioned, and is published, by the Minority Rights Group as a contribution to public understanding of the problem which forms its subject. It does not necessarily represent, in every detail and in all its aspects, the collective view of the Group.

To receive the reports of the Minority Rights Group on a regular basis please take out a subscription. 5 reports annually for £12.00/US$25.

For details of the other reports published by the Minority Rights Group, please see the inside back cover.

Printed by
Expedite Graphic Limited
Murray House, 3 Vandon Street
London SW1H 0AG

The cover photo is of a Maya Indian widow and her child, Quiché province, 1989. (Steve Smith)

THE UNITED NATIONS
UNIVERSAL DECLARATION OF HUMAN RIGHTS

Whereas recognition of the inherent dignity and of the equal and inalienable rights of all members of the human family is the foundation of freedom, justice and peace in the world.

Whereas disregard and contempt for human rights have resulted in barbarous acts which have outraged the conscience of mankind, and the advent of a world in which human beings shall enjoy freedom of speech and belief and freedom from any fear and want has been proclaimed as the highest aspiration of the common people,

Whereas it is essential, if a man is not to be compelled to have recourse, as a last resort, to rebellion against tyranny and oppression, that human rights should be protected by the rule of law,

Whereas it is essential to promote the development of friendly relations between nations,

Whereas the peoples of the United Nations have in the Charter reaffirmed their faith in fundamental human rights, in the dignity and worth of the human person and in the equal rights of men and women and have determined to promote social progress and better standards of life in larger freedom,

Whereas Member States have pledged themselves to achieve, in co-operation with the United Nations, the promotion of universal respect for and observance of human rights and fundamental freedoms,

Whereas a common understanding of these rights and freedoms is of the greatest importance for the full realization of this pledge,

Now, Therefore,

THE GENERAL ASSEMBLY
proclaims

THIS UNIVERSAL DECLARATION OF HUMAN RIGHTS as a common standard of achievement for all peoples and all nations, to the end that every individual and every organ of society, keeping this Declaration constantly in mind, shall strive by teaching and education to promote respect for these rights and freedoms and by progressive measures, national and international, to secure their universal and effective recognition and observance, both among the peoples of Member States themselves and among the peoples of territories under their jurisdiction.

Article 1. All human beings are born free and equal in dignity and rights. They are endowed with reason and conscience and should act towards one another in a spirit of brotherhood.

Article 2. Everyone is entitled to all the rights and freedoms set forth in this Declaration, without distinction of any kind, such as race, colour, sex, language, religion, political or other opinion, national or social origin, property, birth or other status.

Furthermore, no distinction shall be made on the basis of the political, jurisdictional or international status of the country or territory to which a person belongs, whether it be independent, trust, non-self-governing or under any other limitation of sovereignty.

Article 3. Everyone has the right to life, liberty and security of person.

Article 4. No one shall be held in slavery or servitude; slavery and the slave trade shall be prohibited in all their forms.

Article 5. No one shall be subjected to torture or to cruel, inhuman or degrading treatment or punishment.

Article 6. Everyone has the right to recognition everywhere as a person before the law.

Article 7. All are equal before the law and are entitled without any discrimination to equal protection of the law. All are entitled to equal protection against any discrimination in violation of this Declaration and against any incitement to such discrimination.

Article 8. Everyone has the right to an effective remedy by the competent national tribunals for acts violating the fundamental rights granted him by the constitution or by law.

Article 9. No one shall be subjected to arbitrary arrest, detention or exile.

Article 10. Everyone is entitled in full equality to a fair and public hearing by an independent and impartial tribunal, in the determination of his rights and obligations and of any criminal charge against him.

Article 11. (1) Everyone charged with a penal offence has the right to be presumed innocent until proved guilty according to law in a public trial at which he has had all the guarantees necessary for his defence.

(2) No one shall be held guilty of any penal offence on account of any act or omission which did not constitute a penal offence, under national or international law, at the time when it was committed. Nor shall a heavier penalty be imposed than the one that was applicable at the time the penal offence was committed.

Article 12. No one shall be subjected to arbitrary interference with his privacy, family, home or correspondence, nor to attacks upon his honour and reputation. Everyone has the right to the protection of the law against such interference or attacks.

Article 13. (1) Everyone has the right to freedom of movement and residence within the borders of each state.

(2) Everyone has the right to leave any country, including his own, and to return to his country.

Article 14. (1) Everyone has the right to seek and to enjoy in other countries asylum from persecution.

(2) This right may not be invoked in the case of prosecutions genuinely arising from non-political crimes or from acts contrary to the purposes and principles of the United Nations.

Article 15. (1) Everyone has the right to a nationality.

(2) No one shall be arbitrarily deprived of his nationality nor denied the right to change his nationality.

Article 16. (1) Men and women of full age, without any limitation due to race, nationality or religion, have the right to marry and to found a family. They are entitled to equal rights as to marriage, during marriage and at its dissolution.

(2) Marriage shall be entered into only with the free and full consent of the intending spouses.

(3) The family is the natural and fundamental group unit of society and is entitled to protection by society and the State.

Article 17. (1) Everyone has the right to own property alone as well as in association with others.

(2) No one shall be arbitrarily deprived of his property.

Article 18. Everyone has the right to freedom of thought, conscience and religion; this right includes freedom to change his religion or belief, and freedom, either alone or in community with others and in public or private, to manifest his religion or belief in teaching, practice, worship and observance.

Article 19. Everyone has the right to freedom of opinion and expression; this right includes freedom to hold opinions without interference and to seek, receive and impart information and ideas through any media and regardless of frontiers.

Article 20. (1) Everyone has the right to freedom of peaceful assembly and association.

(2) No one may be compelled to belong to an association.

Article 21. (1) Everyone has the right to take part in the government of his country, directly or through freely chosen representatives.

(2) Everyone has the right of equal access to public service in his country.

(3) The will of the people shall be the basis of the authority of government; this will shall be expressed in periodic and genuine elections which shall be by universal and equal suffrage and shall be held by secret vote or by equivalent free voting procedures.

Article 22. Everyone, as a member of society, has the right to social security and is entitled to realization, through national effort and international co-operation and in accordance with the organization and resources of each State, of the economic, social and cultural rights indispensable for his dignity and the free development of his personality.

Article 23. (1) Everyone has the right to work, to free choice of employment, to just and favourable conditions of work and to protection against unemployment.

(2) Everyone, without any discrimination, has the right to equal pay for equal work.

(3) Everyone who works has the right to just and favourable remuneration ensuring for himself and his family an existence worthy of human dignity, and supplemented, if necessary, by other means of social protection.

(4) Everyone has the right to form and to join trade unions for the protection of his interest.

Article 24. Everyone has the right to rest and leisure, including reasonable limitation of working hours and periodic holidays with pay.

Article 25. (1) Everyone has the right to a standard of living adequate for the health and well-being of himself and of his family, including food, clothing, housing and medical care and necessary social services, and the right to security in the event of unemployment, sickness, disability, widowhood, old age or other lack of livelihood in circumstances beyond his control.

(2) Motherhood and childhood are entitled to special care and assistance. All children, whether born in or out of wedlock, shall enjoy the same social protection.

Article 26. (1) Everyone has the right to education. Education shall be free, at least in the elementary and fundamental stages. Elementary education shall be compulsory. Technical and professional education shall be made generally available and higher education shall be equally accessible to all on the basis of merit.

(2) Education shall be directed to the full development of the human personality and to the strengthening of respect for human rights and fundamental freedoms. It shall promote understanding, tolerance and friendship among all nations, racial or religious groups, and shall further the activities of the United Nations for the maintenance of peace.

(3) Parents have a prior right to choose the kind of education that shall be given to their children.

Article 27. (1) Everyone has the right freely to participate in the cultural life of the community, to enjoy the arts and to share in scientific advancement and its benefits.

(2) Everyone has the right to the protection of the moral and material interests resulting from any scientific, literary or artistic production of which he is the author.

Article 28. Everyone is entitled to a social and international order in which the rights and freedoms set forth in this Declaration can be fully realized.

Article 29. (1) Everyone has duties to the community in which alone the free and full development of his personality is possible.

(2) In the exercise of his rights and freedoms, everyone shall be subject only to such limitations as are determined by law solely for the purpose of securing due recognition and respect for the rights and freedoms of others and of meeting the just requirements of morality, public order and the general welfare in a democratic society.

(3) These rights and freedoms may in no case be exercised contrary to the purposes and principles of the United Nations.

Article 30. Nothing in this Declaration may be interpreted as implying for any State, group or person any right to engage in any activity or to perform any act aimed at the destruction of any of the rights and freedoms set forth herein.

Preface

The Mayan peoples of Guatemala are one of the largest concentrations of indigenous peoples in the world. While elsewhere in Central America, the pre-Columbian peoples are now only a small minority, in Guatemala they are probably a majority of the population and have continued to follow a distinctive way of life to the dominant Ladino population. Following the elections of 1985 there were hopes that the civilian government would assert itself and the persecution of the Maya, fully evidenced in MRG's 1984 report, would stop. This report examines allegations that today the Maya are facing the greatest threat to their physical integrity since the 16th century — that of physical and cultural genocide.

The word 'genocide' may seem an emotive one but it also has a precise meaning, defined by the United Nations Convention on the Prevention and Punishment of the Crime of Genocide:

a)   Killing members of a group;
b)   Causing serious bodily or mental harm to members of a group;
c)   Deliberately inflicting on a group conditions of life calculated to bring about its physical destruction;
d)   Imposing measures to prevent births within a group;
e)   Forcibly transferring children of the group to another group.

There is overwhelming evidence that, during the early 1980s, Mayan Indians in Guatemala faced genocidal pressures from Guatemalan military regimes, on the first three counts of the Genocide Convention.

This revised and updated report, *The Maya of Guatemala*, was first published in 1984 under the title *Central America's Indians*. The first edition gave a horrifying account of the three-fold process of killings, cooption and concentration of the Maya; of the slaughter of Indians under the regimes of Generals Lucas García and Ríos Montt, of their incorporation in a civilian militia, and of the beginnings of the 'model village' system.

Phillip Wearne, the author of the Guatemala report, wrote the first edition after extensive travel in Guatemala and the surrounding area. He has continued to work in the region, researching a wide variety of human rights issues in various countries and this, coupled with further visits to Guatemala and to Mexico, temporary home of many refugees, has made him exceptionally well qualified to report on the continuous horrors faced by the Maya.

Guatemala must be seen in the context of Central America as a whole. This report includes an overview by Professor Peter Calvert of the University of Southampton, an acknowledged expert on the politics of the region. For a more detailed account of the situation in Nicaragua, the reader should look at MRG Report No 79, *The Miskito Indians of Nicaragua*, by Dr Roxanne Dunbar Ortiz, published in September 1988.

When this report was first published it was one of the few publications which concentrated explicitly on the situation of the Indians, combining history, anthropology and human rights. This new edition continues these themes, demonstrating the continuing place of the Indian at the very bottom of Guatemalan society. It shows how the Maya face racial discrimination, poverty and abuse and how the current economic crisis has hit Indians hardest with real incomes falling precipitously in the last decade. Access to land remains the root of the problem with hundreds of thousands of Indians being forced to migrate to coastal plantations to harvest cash crops in unacceptable conditions for less than adequate wages.

Yet as this report shows, even here there are changes. Indians are fighting back, not with guns but with their combined strength and together with poor Ladinos within Guatemala. Organizations fighting against death squads, for human rights, for material support for the victims and for the ownership and control of land, have been formed in recent years. Mayan representatives have been elected to the Constituent Assembly and are working hard to push indigenous issues up the political agenda. Progressive development agencies and the Catholic and some Protestant churches have been active in assisting community organization and material support in Guatemala and the refugee camps. All these efforts require international awareness and support and this is one of the reasons for publishing again on this important issue.

The year 1992 will mark 500 years since the landing by the European explorer Christopher Columbus in the Caribbean and the beginnings of European domination and exploitation of the Americas. For the indigenous inhabitants it was the end of their traditional ways of life. In the islands they were almost entirely exterminated. The process did not reach Guatemala until the 1520s but there it was slightly cushioned by the fact that the society the Spanish conquistadores introduced had some structural similarities to that of the Mayan rulers. Nevertheless Indians suffered terribly and since that time have chosen to submit, adapt and survive rather than be wiped out confronting a superior force. Today Indian life and culture is again under attack throughout the Americas, whether from repressive governments, multinational companies or environmental destruction. The Maya of Guatemala are part of that continuing struggle to survive.

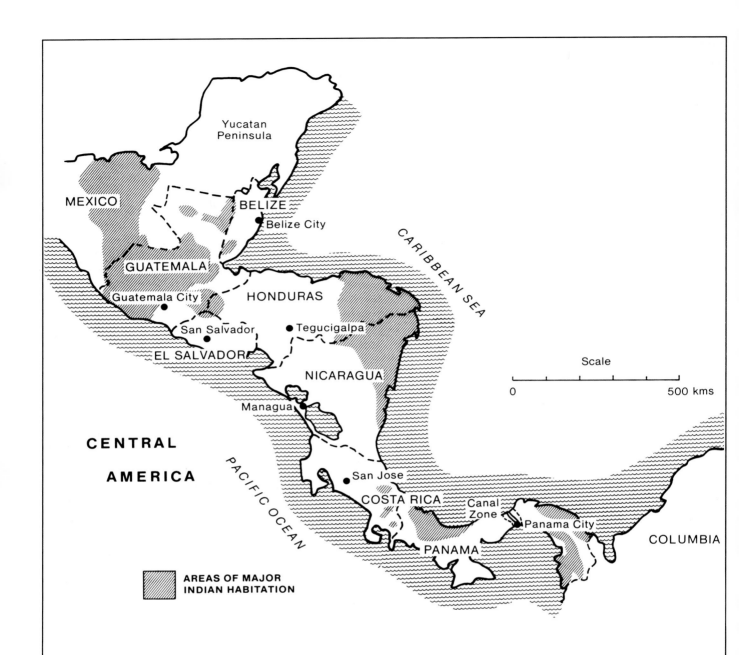

AREAS OF MAJOR INDIAN HABITATION

Central America — A Quick Reference

	Area in sq km	Total Population	Population Density/sq km	Estimate of Ethnic Indian Population★		% of Total Population
Guatemala	108,889	7,100,000	65	2,700,000	(official	38%
				3,600,000	plus (unofficial)	50% plus
Belize	22,963	150,000	6.5	15,000		10%
Honduras	112,088	3,595,000	32	250,000		7%
El Salvador	21,393	4,813,000	225	960,000		20%
Nicaragua	148,000 (surface area: 130,000)	2,733,000	18 (21)	135,000		5%
Costa Rica	50,900	2,286,000	45	20,000		0.1%
Panama	75,650	1,830,000	24	100,000		5%

★ includes those of mixed Afro-Caribbean-Carib descent (e.g. in Belize: Maya; Ketchi; Garifuna)

(population figures from 1984)

PART I – CENTRAL AMERICA'S INDIANS
by Peter Calvert

In retrospect it is clear 1978 was a turning point in history of the indigenous peoples of Central America. It was the year in which the Panzós massacre in Guatemala ushered in a full-scale race war between the armed forces of the government and the Indian population of the North-east and North-west, and in which the assassination of an opposition leader touched off the Nicaraguan Revolution which resulted in the fall of the Somozas and the establishment of the Sandinista government, which in turn inspired revolution in El Salvador, and brought in retaliation the intervention of the United States to oust the Sandinista government.

This report is not concerned with the position of the Indians within Nicaragua, which is the subject of a separate report.[1] However the existence of the conflict has necessarily had repercussions on the safety and welfare of Indian groups north of the frontier with Honduras and the inability to restore peace in the region is integrally bound up with the US refusal to accept any solution short of the fall of the Sandinista government.

Overview

Central America was heavily populated at the time of the Spanish conquest, but otherwise it was a disappointment to the conquistadores, because it lacked gold and silver. After the initial expeditions of Pedro de Alvarado and others, it became a backward area within the Spanish Empire, attracting few European settlers and producing few export products of any value other than wood, hides and tallow. The Maya city of Tayasal in the Yucatán peninsula (now Flores, in El Petén, Guatemala) remained isolated and did not fall to the Spaniards until 1697. The impact of Spanish colonization in the region was therefore relatively slight, and the excess of Spanish males over females so great that intermarriage was common from the outset.

The Spaniards did not practise indirect rule and in theory imposed their own form of government. However because there were so few Spaniards, Indian tribal and village structures remained largely intact, 'encapsulated' within Hispanic society. Indians were however made to work for their conquerors. Nominally their labour was for the Crown only, but venal governors allowed their services to be transferred to private landowners in return for a consideration. Cheap labour saved Spaniards from having to work the fields and gave them a standard of living few could have aspired to at home. They took the best lands wherever they could, and with them the services of their existing inhabitants, leaving the remaining Indian communities to work marginal land for their subsistence as they had always done.

At Independence in 1821 the liberal leaders of Central America decreed an end to slavery. But Central America failed to maintain its unity and split into five separate states, when in 1838 an illiterate mule driver, Rafael Carrera, seized power as the first independent ruler of Guatemala. Like him, many if not most of the 19th century presidents and dictators of the region had Indian blood, but under the prevailing system of ideas they sought to be 'European' rulers and tended to view manifestations of Indian culture as at best quaint survivals and at worst as evidence of incorrigible backwardness that had to be stamped out. Spanish was the sole official language of politics, law and business and nowhere in Central America was any Indian language recognized. In the name of the most advanced ideas of their time, the more able of the rulers of the period sought to develop their countries on Liberal principles, such as Justo Rufino Barrios in Guatemala creating a new plantation agriculture based on coffee. But in turn this gave rise to a new system of compulsory work. Until 1911, when the US first emerged as the hegemonic power of the Caribbean region, these rulers spent much of the resources of their poverty-stricken states trying to subdue their neighbours and to reunify Central America.

Many Central Americans still feel the region ought to be reunited. If US intervention put an end to conflict, however, it also put an end to any serious chance of unification. After 1921 US governments preferred to deal with the individual states and in the 1930s all but Costa Rica fell prey to dictatorships. Only after World War II was social progress renewed, initially regarded with suspicion and then encouraged after the success of the Cuban Revolution in 1959. The last serious attempt to date at reunification was the creation of the Central American Common Market (CACM) in 1961. This increased intra-regional trade by three times in seven years. But migration from small and overcrowded El Salvador into sparsely populated Honduras exacerbated traditional boundary tensions and CACM stopped working after a brief 13-day war in 1969 (the 'Football War') had led to more than 2000 casualties and resulted in the withdrawal of Honduras from active membership. By the time a peace treaty had been signed in 1980, the region was again in turmoil following the Nicaraguan Revolution of 1979, and the outbreak of civil war in El Salvador itself.

Economically the area remains backward, tied too closely for comfort to the growth of single crops for export, and subject to the periodic disasters of hurricane and earthquake. Inevitably the US, as it rose from a regional to a world superpower, came to dominate the economies of the regional states, and bananas grown for export to the US became the foundation for a vertical operation of huge local importance and the power of the former United Fruit Company of Boston. Since that time there has been huge growth in other export crops, notably coffee and cotton. Unification as a single market would be very desirable from the purely economic point of view, even though the economies tend to be competitive and not complementary. But economic development in Central America has for the past century been closely tied to the incorporation of the Indians in the modern sector of the economy and to the steady erosion of their distinctive way of life.

Panama, before 1903 part of Colombia, is regarded geographically as part of South America, although comparable with the Central American Republics in size and social problems. The choice of Panama as the route for the long dreamed of interoceanic Canal, which was finished and opened in 1914, is still its principal reason for existence as an independent state and places it at the centre of US strategic interests in the Caribbean Basin. With the US now a world superpower, its power in the area would seem unchallengeable. For US policymakers however the 1980s have seen Central America take centre stage, as fears grew that Cuba (and behind them the Soviet Union) was exploiting latent unrest to gain a world strategic advantage. The Nicaraguan Revolution was originally regarded with suspicion and the Carter Administration tried to forestall it. Then civil war broke out in neighbouring El Salvador, which was attributed by the incoming Reagan Administration not to the endemic poverty and inequality, but to communist strategic designs on the hemisphere. Though the same view is not shared by other Latin American states, fears that unrest would spread to neighbouring states were shared by their governments, who see US involvement as the problem, not the solution. These concerns lie behind two major plans to bring peace to the region: the *Contadora Plan* (1983), sponsored by Mexico, Panama, Colombia and Venezuela, and the *Arias Plan* (1986), mooted by President Oscar Arias of Costa Rica, and accepted by the governments of all the Central American states.

Indian consciousness

Contrary to practice in some other parts of the world, the term 'native' (*indigena* in Spanish) is not always regarded as derogatory and has indeed been adopted by moderate Indian movements as a badge of pride in their distinctive culture and traditions. 'Indian' itself was long regarded as derogatory but was revived by the Peruvian political leader Victor Haya de la Torre in the 1930s and has recently been adopted by radical groups who see their struggle as being one for national liberation.

Indigenismo as a political movement for the revival of interest in and development of the status of Indian culture originated in the Andean region in the late 19th century. It received a powerful boost from the rediscovery of Mexico's pre-Columbian roots during the Mexican Revolution (1910-40), and in 1948 the Interamerican Native Congress held in Cuzco, Peru, formally defined the Indian as 'the descendant of pre-Columbian nations and peoples who shares a social awareness and a lifestyle — recognizable to his own people as well as to outsiders - - in his system of work, in his language and in his traditions even where they have undergone some modification through outside contacts'.[2]

The *indigenista* revival was late to reach Central America and the first international conference of Central American Indians was held as recently as 1977 in Panama, leading to the creation of a permanent bureau, the Regional Council of Indigenous Peoples of Central America (CORPI). There as elsewhere however it has been complicated by a fundamental dispute about the nature of Indianism and how *indigenista* aspirations should be resolved. The dispute stems from the fact that being an Indian is not simply a matter of descent but a matter of culture and economic status: the word 'Indian' therefore denotes both what has been loosely termed 'race' and what can be called 'class'. An Indian who wears native dress and sandals (*huaraches*) and eats maize will be regarded as an Indian; the same individual who wears European clothes and eats wheaten bread will be regarded as a Ladino. Marxists from José Carlos Mariátegui onwards have argued that Indians are a class and that liberation of the Indian is the process of being freed from economic subjection through social revolution. Culturalists have argued that Indians are not a class but a distinctive group bound by their own traditions and culture and that their liberation must therefore come from within. Since 1980 it is the latter view that has become dominant among *indigenista* movements in the region. The problem is that it does not resolve the fundamental difficulty that both views are to some extent correct. In Central America Indians are at the bottom of the social class ladder, and where present, the Caribbean blacks and Chinese settlers rank above them.

The Central American States

The Central American states are here grouped according to the classification used by the 1977 Declaration of Barbados, which divided Indians into three groups:

1. those who had remained more or less isolated and had conserved their own cultures,

2. those who still conserve much of their culture but are incorporated into the capitalist economic system,

3. those who have been de-indianized by 'integral forces'.

1. States in which pockets of Indian culture remain intact:

BELIZE The newcomer to the area, Belize, formerly a British colony but independent since 1981, is a parliamentary democracy whose Prime Minister, George Price, took over from the government of Manuel Esquivel after elections in September 1989. His country, unfortunately, has still to be recognized by its neighbour Guatemala, which has trimmed its traditional claims to its whole territory but remains a potential threat. Guatemala's army alone is more than a fifth of the size of Belize's entire population, most of which consists of English-speaking Caribbean blacks. Indians make up about 10% of the population. Both blacks and Indians cross the border freely in both directions in normal circumstances, and Belizean Indians are mostly Kekchi and Mopan, recent refugees from Guatemala. A small defence force is being trained by the UK to provide token protection and Britain retains a 'trip-wire' force in the country pending resolution of the boundary dispute.

COSTA RICA For a hundred years an oasis of democracy in Central America, it is rightly said there is nowhere like Costa Rica. Rich volcanic soil, relatively evenly distributed, is the secret alike of its fine coffee (its major export) and of its stable social structure. The majority of the population are of European descent, with small numbers of Indians (less than 0.1%) and blacks. The abolition of the armed forces in 1948 by the far-sighted José Figueres and his colleagues has so far kept it free from the scourge of militarism. Power changes hands by free elections which are keenly contested. Educational levels are high by regional standards and poverty rare. Long term stability, however, lies in strict neutrality and keeping out of regional conflicts, and US pressures to rearm, however well-intentioned, are seen as a threat to its unique way of life.

HONDURAS Neglected by Spain and still sparsely populated, a large part of Honduras remains isolated even today. The major export crop, bananas, were and continue to be grown in an enclave of US enterprise on the north coast linked by the country's few railways to the ports of Tela and San Pedro Sula. Although small by US standards, the banana interests have been overwhelmingly powerful by Honduran standards — in 1975 a President fell because it was revealed he had accepted a bribe of $500,000 to keep banana prices down. The population is mainly of mixed blood, with some 7% regarded as ethnic Indians, mainly Sumo and Miskito-speaking, and a substantial population of blacks on the Caribbean coast. From December 1981 many Miskito moved northward from Nicaragua as refugees although since 1987 large numbers have returned to the Atlantic coast of Nicaragua.

Once a backwater, over the years Honduras, linked to North and South by the Pan American Highway, has assumed increasing strategic significance. The US backed 'contras' operate over the border into revolutionary Nicaragua and since 1984 US troops, currently numbering some 50,000, have been stationed in the country, officially on exercises. The Honduran Army, traditionally reticent in politics, is torn between the economic advantages of continued involvement in the long-running dispute and its fears for the future. Growth is being promoted by US investment in the transport infrastructure but its future is uncertain. Meanwhile isolated Indian communities have been brought into contact with a modern society which previously they could largely ignore.

PANAMA Panama is the Canal; its other sources of revenue, flags of convenience and offshore banking, depend on its unique position at a crossroads of world trade, and even its cosmopolitan population is the product of its position — ethnic Indians account for under 5% of its population. But the Canal (like Panama) was the creation of the US, which under the 1977 Treaties retains a controlling interest in it until 31 December 1999. Deforestation (blamed for declining rainfall), silting and the size of modern supertankers combine to make the future of the present Canal and its elaborate locks problematic, but agreement on a possible replacement remains to be reached.

Deforestation and silting are both products of a programme of internal colonization which has brought settlers into lands previously isolated, and so threaten the independent future of the Guaymi and Kuna Indians. The completion of the Panamerican Highway through the marshes of the Darien Gap will bring North and South America together for the first time by land transport — potentially at least as meaningful a development as the Canal itself. But the price will be the incorporation of Panama's last nomadic groups in the country's internationalist culture.

Behind the settlers, as elsewhere in the region, stands the armed force of the government. Though Panama is nominally a presidential democracy, in practice the Defence Forces (still often called the National Guard) call all the shots. The US has tried and failed to dislodge their commander, General Noriega, despite their accusations that he has long been involved in the international drug traffic.

2. State in which Indian culture is substantially incorporated into the modern sector:

GUATEMALA Guatemala is about the size of Greece. Like Greece, too, it was once the centre of a major world civilization. Indians form a majority of the population. It remains primarily an Indian society, with Indian languages such as Quiché and Pokomam still widely spoken. A decade ago more than half the population could be regarded as Indian, though official figures placed the proportion at just 38%. But the Indians' ancestors were driven off the best lands on to the less productive uplands, and land reforms, frustrated in the 1950s, remains a bitter issue. After a century and a half of almost unbroken dictatorship, the government elected in 1986 for a four year term, though nominally headed by a civilian, the Christian Democrat, Vinicio Cerezo Arévalo, survives only by grace of the Army. It helps that the President is a black belt at Judo and never travels without a small armoury of weapons, all of which he knows how to use.

For the 'Land of Eternal Spring' is torn by bitter and seemingly irreconcileable tensions and although Guatemala is the one country in the region with an Indian majority its future and that of its culture is under threat from two sides: physical attack from military or military- backed government bent on the internal colonization of the country and economic attack from the growing scarcity of land amongst the Indian communities and the effects of their growing involvement in a modernizing economy.

In 1978 the military government of President Romeo Lucas Garcia turned the armed forces loose on the civil population in an effort to stamp out the persistent guerrilla activity which had been endemic in the southern uplands since the early 1960s. The consequences were catastrophic. Believing that their greatest danger lay in uncontrolled movement in the high mountainous region on the Mexican border, search and destroy operations in the North-Western departments rapidly escalated into a systematic campaign of extermination directed from the Presidential Palace. In 1982 Lucas Garcia was overthrown and a fundamentalist Protestant, Colonel Efrain Rios Montt, assumed power, promising liberalization and a new approach to the Indian 'problem'. Within weeks the soldiers were again active in the countryside, enforcing the new policy of 'beans and bullets' (*fusiles y frijoles*), meaning that communities prepared to form self-defence organizations would be given food and the means to defend themselves. Though his religious views led to his overthrow in a further coup, his policy of forcible incorporation of the Indian population in a military-dominated Ladino society was continued by his successor, General Oscar Mejia Victores, whose watchword was 'We must get rid of the words "indigenous" and "Indian".' Inevitably the traditional structures of Indian society suffered grievously and tens of thousands died in the North-Western and North-Eastern Departments at the hands of the armed forces and their auxiliaries, the death squads.

Indian society was already threatened, even in the picturesque tourist area around Lake Aititlán, by growing land scarcity which had driven an increasing number of peasant cultivators to journey down into the lowlands to work as seasonal labourers. By 1970 some 90% of rural Indian families did not own their own land or owned less than the 7 ha. considered necessary to support them. The largest economy in Central America, Guatemala still depends to an unhealthy degree on exports of primary agricultural products, especially coffee. Cotton has been the most successful of the new crops, but the heavy use of aerial crop-dusting has given rise to repeated complaints that migratory workers have been subjected to excessive doses of harmful chemicals. Forestry has expanded drastically in the last decade, but the ecological consequences are worrying and the new roads driven through the forest are destroying the remaining forest areas on which the Indian communities depend. The late 1970s saw Guatemala's unexpected transformation into a significant oil producer, with a substantial surplus for export. The social effect has been to exacerbate the struggle over land in the north west highlands, although the discoveries have given a further boost to the diversification of the economy. Over the last decade the position of the Indian in Guatemala has deteriorated to the point at which the separate existence of Indian culture now hangs in the balance. If the trend continues, by the end of the century Guatemala's Indian communities may have ceased to exist except for tourist purposes. In the meanwhile, however, revived Indian consciousness remains a new and highly unpredictable element in the life of Guatemala.

3. State in which Indians have been 'de-indianized':

EL SALVADOR Smallest of the traditional states of Central America but the most densely populated, some 20% of its population were still regarded as ethnic Indians at the start of the 1980s, but El Salvador's traditional Indian culture has been almost wholly eroded by the pressures of plantation agriculture and nearly a decade of civil war. Since 1980, when left-wingers sought to emulate events in neighbouring Nicaragua but failed to take power, US backing for the armed forces has been effective in bringing a stalemate and the insurgents have been prepared to talk. US support for a democratic outcome has foundered on the weakness of the political centre, and the public intransigence of the extreme right, which shocked world opinion by the assassination at Mass of Archbishop Romero in 1980. In 1989 the civilian President José Napoleón Duarte, though dying from cancer, successfully completed his term, but his successor, Sr. Cristiani, was elected by the hard-right Arena party and fear is rife of a campaign of violence in the countryside like that which devastated Guatemala in the late 1970s.

Conclusion

The overall picture for Indian cultures in Central America, therefore, is bleak. A general settlement of the conflicts that have torn the region apart in the 1980s is urgent if creeping militarization and the homogenization of the societies of the region, both by force and the effects of uncontrolled economic pressures, is to be arrested.

FOOTNOTES TO PART I

[1] *The Miskito Indians of Nicaragua*, MRG Report No. 79, by Roxanne Dunbar Ortiz, 1988, pp 7-8.

[2] Quoted by David Stephen in *Central America's Indians*, MRG Report No. 62, 1984 (now out of print), p 3.

Table 1
Language Groups of the Guatemalan Maya

Maya Language Group	Number of Speakers (ca. 1973)
Achi of Cubulco	18,000
Aguacateco	16,000
Akateko	8,000
Cakchiquel	405,000
Chortí	52,000
Chuj	29,000
Itzá	1,000
Ixil	71,000
Jacalteco	32,000
Kanjobal	112,000
Kekchi	361,000
Mam	644,000
Maya-Mopan	5,000
Pocomán	32,000
Pokomchí	50,000
Quiché	967,000
Rabinal Achí	40,000
Sacapulteco	21,000
Sipacapense	3,000
Tacaneco	42,000
Tectiteco	2,500
Tzutujil	80,000
Uspanteco	2,000

Source: *Bibliografia del Instituto Lingüístico de Verano de Centroamérica*, edited by Pamela Sheetz de Echerd (Guatemala City: Instituto de Verano, 1983), 4-7.

PART II – GUATEMALA by Phillip Wearne

1. Who are the Indians? A definition:

'An historical definition of a Guatemalan Indian is easy', commented one anthropologist in the course of this study. 'Deciding who is one today, is not.'

Guatemala's Indians are, as they refer to themselves, the nation's indigenous or 'natural' people. They are the pure-blooded descendants of the Mayan architects of the 'lost' jungle cities of Central America, builders of such a classic civilization that one archaeologist has described them (rather ethnocentrically) as 'the most brilliant aboriginal people on the planet.'[1] Despite the total cultural dominance of Guatemala's other main ethnic group, the Ladino (of mixed Spanish and indigenous descent) the nation's Indians have maintained much of their Mayan heritage. While Spanish is the official language the indigenous people still speak in the glottal stops of a dialect of one of the 22 Mayan languages used. Though conquered in the name of Christianity, many Indians still perform Mayan ritual worship at shrines in the mountains. Indigenous *shamans* (medicine men, magicians, diviners) still count 13 months of 20 days on one of the three Mayan calendars and many Indians wear one of over 100 brightly-coloured, home-woven costumes bearing designs related to the hieroglyphic symbols on Mayan stelae.

Yet history does not define an Indian today. Some anthropologists have argued in the past that the essential criteria are biological and racial, but all now seem to agree that culture and language are the essential criteria. 'The criteria are a little subjective', says one Guatemalan census official. 'We ask the subjects' neighbours if they're indigenous, then consider dress, language, and general socio-economic condition.' This problem of definition has resulted in widely differing estimates of the proportion of Indians in the population of Guatemala. John D. Early's survey numbered the country's Mayan people at 3,230,393 or 47.3% of the total in 1980 (see table 1) although independent estimates range up to 65%.

The problem in essence is that no one single cultural criterion is definitive. Racially, many Ladinos have the dark brown skin and hairless features of the Guatemalan Indian. Geographically, Guatemala's indigenous people are not confined to the western *altiplano* (highlands) as is generally thought. Although overwhelmingly rural, living in the smallest units of settlement — *aldeas* (villages) and *caserios* (hamlets) — they inter-mix with Ladinos even there. Neither language nor dress is a definitive criterion. Many Indians speak perfect Spanish, albeit as a second language, and only a minority of men, though not women, now sport Indian dress. In short, there are broad areas of cultural overlap; as one anthropologist concluded about many customs, 'there are differences only of degree.'[2] Yet these are obvious. Indigenous men and women squat on the ground; Ladinos sit on chairs. Indian men carry loads on their backs by means of a leather headstrap, the *mecapal*; Ladinos don't. But, ultimately, there is, as observers have noted, more to being an Indian than outward characteristics. Perception and outlook on the world are probably the only criteria that allow 22 often widely different groups to be classified together as Indian yet apart from the Ladino.

'Traditionally it has always been more important for the Indian to be somebody rather than have something', is how one experienced indigenous observer put it. 'How he is seen by his neighbours is vital.' Indigenous thinking is undoubtedly marked by less materialistic, and to some extent less individualistic, qualities than the Ladino's Western-orientated outlook. Digital watches and cassette recorders,

LOCATION OF MAYAN GROUPS IN GUATEMALA

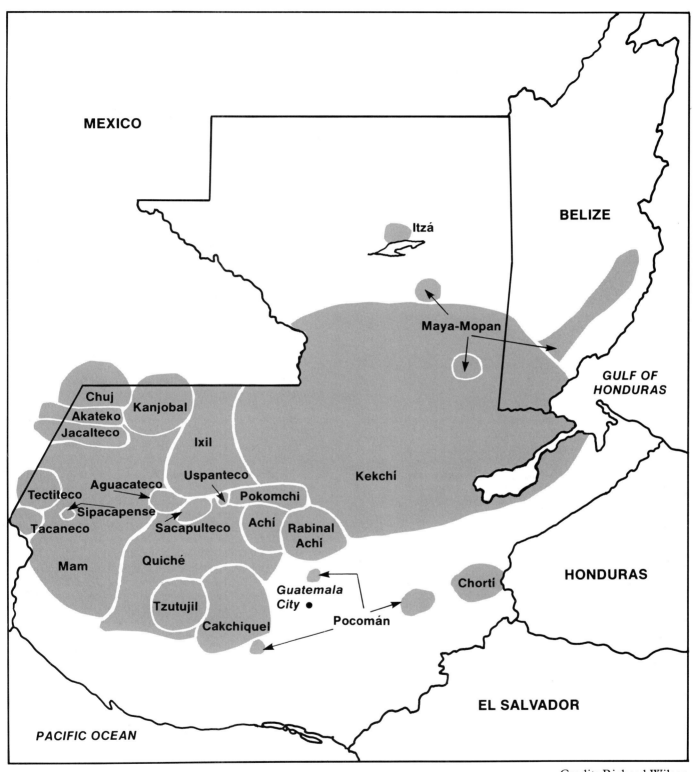

MEXICO

Itzá

BELIZE

Maya-Mopan

GULF OF
HONDURAS

Chuj

Kanjobal

Akateko

Jacalteco

Ixil

Uspanteco

Tectiteco

Aguacateco

Pokomchi

Kekchí

Sipacapense

Sacapulteco

Achí

Tacaneco

Rabinal
Achí

Mam

Quiché

HONDURAS

Chortí

Guatemala
City ●

Tzutujil

Pocomán

Cakchiquel

EL SALVADOR

PACIFIC OCEAN

though highly desirable, are not deemed to be all important. 'A Ladino of whatever category will not live in a *rancho* (Indian hut) if he can afford a house . . . such cannot be said with equal certainty about indigenous people.'[3] Such desire as there is for economic success is usually linked to increasing prestige and respect in the community and must meet strict requirements. 'Approval is given only if the person's activity is regarded as honourable and not exploitative. A person who uses his work position to take unfair advantage is severely criticized as *mala gente* (bad person)', notes the same writer.

Respect, responsibility, honesty and hard work are the traditional indigenous values that have been woven into a code from which there was little individual deviation. Within this code striving and competition were unnecessary, one writer noted, as 'everyone who follows patterns and precepts received status sometime during life'.[4] Such respect and status have traditionally been won by community service in a system of religious brotherhoods known as *cofradías*. Positions and respective responsibilities vary considerably but cofradías were always age-grade hierarchies that served social and political functions as well as their patron saint. As teenagers, members would perform menial tasks like sweeping the market-place or running messages; *alguaciles* in their late teens or early twenties served as village policemen. In their forties and fifties, a member might expect to become cofrade himself or a *regidor* (councilman) and finally *alcalde* (mayor) but only after serving the prescribed year at every level. *Principales,* old men who have graduated through the whole system, were the ultimate overseers, maintaining the vital links with the ancestors simply by virtue of their age and experience in the local *costumbres* (traditions) that governed the whole structure.

Land ownership, and attitudes towards it, is another major facet of indigenous outlook. The vast majority of Guatemalan Indians are subsistence farmers, so their tiny plots of mountainous land (or *milpas*), are vital for the maize, beans and squash that are Indian staples. But, land means much more. Firstly, it is identity. A *milpa* is an Indian's 'symbol of his right to live'.[5] For many, being a *milpero* (subsistence farmer) is an essential symbol of 'Indianness', not just because Indians were all traditionally farmers but because without it one usually had to leave the village and thus sever the ties that are the basis of one's cultural identity.

Inheritance from father to son means that land is a vital link with one's ancestors and thus represents an Indian's personal as well as cultural identity. Land is *who*, as well as *what*, he is. Land also represents virility — ability to provide for children both as dependents (food) and adults (inheritance). Many predominately indigenous areas also have a system of common land cultivation which reinforces the communal identity of individual towns, villages and linguistic groups. Land which may pass down from one family generation to another is often actually on a sort of indeterminate lease from the local authorities and can be redistributed as the need arises.

Secondly, land has religious significance. The land is the home of the most important Indian god, the omnipotent *Dios Mundo* (earth god). A traditional Indian will consult a Mayan *shaman* on when to start any major part of the agricultural cycle, begin it with religious ceremonies in the milpa itself, and apologize to the ground before breaking it, in an effort to appease *Dios Mundo*. Cultivating the land is the most profound communion with God an Indian can aspire to.

Thirdly, land produces the almost sacred ear of maize, whose flour is patted into the *tortillas* (flat maize pancakes) that are the basis of every meal. Traditional indigenous belief maintains that if they do not eat maize flour they will

somehow lose their 'Indianness' and a legend of the Quiché Indians preserved in the sacred Popol Vul records how the first men were moulded of corn paste, an ideal substance after 'The Makers' had rejected mud as too soft and wood as being too hard.

Perhaps more than any other attribute it is the Guatemalan Indian's attachment to the land which remains intact today. It is amply illustrated by stories about a wealthy Indian businessman who returns to his village and *milpa* in a suit every planting season and of the indigenous guerrilla fighters who deserted the revolution because it was harvest time. Many too, are the Indian economic refugees in Mexico and the US whose sole aim is to return to Guatemala with sufficient funds to buy land.

A third facet of the Indian outlook is an all-pervading sense of the religious, magical and supernatural. 'Animals talk, plants have emotions, it is possible for a hoe to work alone; . . . ghosts are always abroad; the soul of a person leaves his body for hours or days while he still lives. These are not simply superstitions, they are part of the life of the community and normally taken into consideration in determining courses of action.'[6] Central to these beliefs are the shamans or *Aj K'ijs* who divine, cure, interpret and advise, operating with much ritual by means of various pieces of jadeite or obsidian, beans, seeds and copal, an Indian incense. Most significantly, these shamans have inherited the traditions of the ancient Mayan priests and observe the 260-day religious calendar called the Sacred Round of Tzolkin. Each day in the thirteen 20-day months is given a name, deity, such as Jaguar (*in Quiché Ix*) or Monkey (*Batz*), and number from one to thirteen. The combination of these decides the day's power for good or evil. 'The day is the only way to decide what sickness the patient has', a *shaman* confided to this writer. God is everywhere in nature in traditional Indian belief and is thus worshipped in rituals at shrines, on rivers, up mountains and in other venerated places. Animals and nature command love and respect as personifications of God, the sun and the earth being the most powerful. Many Indians pay their respects to the sun by genuflecting to it at dawn, and 'Don't Fall!', the literal goodbye of several Indian languages, reflects the hope that you will not offend the Earth God by tumbling on him, as much as the perils of walking the mountain trails that lace Indian areas.

This all-pervading religious sense and curious logic applies to medicine, the other main concern of the *shaman*. 'Health to us is the absence of disease. Health to an Indian is a sense of fulfilment or well-being.'[7] According to several doctors who have worked with Indians, their routine, established codes of behaviour and task-simple culture amount to a psychological contentment which generates this sense of fulfilment. 'The Indian is less violent and less prone to anger', says one. Their emotional balance is reflected in the almost total lack of accidents they have, even when using dangerous tools like machetes and axes.' This 'total', relative concept of health leads to a shock being equated to a 'loss of soul' when an Indian feels 'spiritually' sick. Physical illness itself is often broken down to an imbalance of hot and cold forces in the body. 'We are strictly trained to draw certain conclusions from certain data. The Indian has an equally strict, and to him logical, interpretation of the same data, quite alien to us', observed one Ladino doctor.[8] Yet, the perception is always logical — according to another physician, 'Indian mothers give babies coffee instead of breast-feeding. Of course — give it "maternal milk" and it gets drowsy and seems sick. Give it coffee and it perks up and, logically, is well.'

Such Indian perceptions and values are apparently fundamentally irreconcilable with those of Ladino society. Yet somehow both Indians and Ladinos have co-existed for centuries, if not always peacefully, at least as separate cultural identities. Why?

Historically, potential culture shock was cushioned by the fact that the society the Spanish conquistadores introduced had many structural similarities to that of the indigenous people. For the vast majority of Indians the Spanish hierarchy just took the place of the Mayan lords and priests. The saints the new priests introduced became personifications of the deities already worshipped, while the cross had always represented eternal life and the four cardinal points in Mayan religion. Since the conquest, the Indian has chosen to survive rather than be wiped out by confronting a superior force. Over the centuries submission has moulded the indigenous character and its symptoms are obvious today. Despite ethics which value honesty many Indians tend to tell outsiders what they think they want to hear as a result of years of trying to please the *patrón*. From this apparent subjugation and cultural conquest Guatemala's indigenous people have moulded a very adapted, but still essentially Indian, way of life. If today's Indian dress was imposed by the Spanish, as many maintain, it is now a symbol of ethnic pride, not submission. Surnames imposed by the conquistadores have been 'indianized'. The *cofradías* and individual land ownership, both originally imposed, are now pillars of indigenous society.

Adapt and survive. Hope for change in the future, but in the meantime adapt and survive. These are probably the most obvious — and essential — indigenous traits, both in the past and present. Only in the light of this process can we understand the Indian's position in Guatemalan society today.

2. Discrimination: The Indian's place in Guatemalan society

Guatemala City is full of government officials who, when asked about the nation's indigenous people, will relate how the Indians were parcelled out with *encomiendas* (royal land grants) as virtual slaves, herded into *congregaciónes* (settlements) as a means of control, stripped of their lands and forcibly 'civilized'.

But although today's officials might admit to a little 'discrimination', none will admit that the structure of Guatemalan society is essentially the same today — 'endo-colonial' since independence from Spain in 1821, according to one commentator;[9] more colonial, according to another. According to the latter, many *criollos* (Spanish descendents) saw independence as 'the only way of eliminating impediments such as regulations on the treatment of Indian labour'.[10] Social structure, laws and attitudes since independence seem to bear this out.

One observer has stratified Guatemala's ethnic hierarchy thus: a small elite of white Europeans at the top, followed by a group of mixed bloods known as *Guatemaltecos*, urban Ladinos, followed by rural Ladinos with Indians firmly at the bottom.[11] Carib blacks, centered around Livingstone on the Atlantic Coast, and a sizeable Chinese community have to be fitted into this hierarchy somewhere — but certainly not below Indians. 'It's better to be black than Indian', several objective informants told this writer.

The ethnic pecking order matches the socio-economic pyramid almost exactly. Europeans are wealthy industrialists and agro-export businessmen with big ranches to their names. *Guatemaltecos* tend to be professionals, military officers, lesser industrialists and farm owners, with urban Ladinos being petty bourgeois business people or white collar employees, and their rural counterparts small scale farmers. Indians are sub-subsistence farmers, 'penny' merchants, migratory farm workers and, in urban contexts, servants, maids, factory staff and construction workers.

Ethnic discrimination is very basic in Guatemalan society, as a few questions to almost any Ladino will testify. Inevitably, it takes many forms. The Indian is ignored at government hospitals, overcharged in Ladino shops and buses, sent to the back of any queue. But it's Ladino comments that say most about the nation's racial discrimination. Indians are dirty, lazy, indolent and, above all, primitive or backward. They need 'civilizing', in short, Ladinoizing. 'You can't teach the Indians anything. How many times have we tried to improve their way of life, but they won't change', says one Ladino.[12]

But the attitude runs deeper. Not content with labelling Indians '*inditos*' — itself an insult — Ladinos often equate Indians with animals or other sub-humans in what is probably a reflection of early *conquistador* doubts about the humanity of indigenous peoples. 'If you're not careful you will be ruled by the "mules" (the Indians)', one Ladino warned some younger colleagues.[13] 'They're not children, they're Indians', one ranch owner's daughter recalls being told by her father, when worrying about an outbreak of coughing among Indian labourer's children.[14]

But Guatemala's racism is made particularly insidious by the thin veneer of equality proclaimed by the state. The 1985 constitution forbids discrimination on the basis of race, colour, economic or social condition while four Articles on the subject of indigenous communities recognize every form of indigenous right and even commit the state to providing the land considered necessary for indigenous communities to 'develop'.[15]

As part of this government policy of pretence there are two small government departments concerned with indigenous people. The National Indigenous Institute (IIN) was founded in 1945 and run through most of the 1980s by six investigators who researched and published numerous reports. However, as one employee told this writer in 1983: 'No recommendations are made and there is never any action.' Indeed, the government didn't seem to have noticed the Institute until its spending attracted attention in 1988 and it was downgraded to a department of the Ministry of Culture in August of that year. The Service for the Development of the Indian Economy is even more suspect, its aims being that repeatedly hinted at by the Constitution — the incorporation of indigenous people into 'national' life.

Perhaps even more objectionable is both the states' and private interests' exploitation of elements of indigenous culture. The government's IIN's slogan refers to Indian culture as 'the base of our nationality'. In 1976 the Guatemalan government entered an Indian Ixil costume for the Miss Universe native costume competition. 'Guatemala' won with a white-skinned model displaying the Ixil women's ceremonial *huipil* (embroidered overblouse). The Mayan numbering system and the Quiché Indian chief Tecún Umán, who was killed fighting off the conquistador invaders, appear on national bank notes and — in the most macabre irony — numerous Indians have been killed by a regiment named after the Mayan god of war. Indians decorate tourist posters, postcards, and even advertisements. In short, they are used whenever there's some advantage in terms of international recognition or financial profit.

The basis of Guatemalan racism appears to be fear and greed — a classic complex of a rich exploitative group that has inherited a subconscious paranoia as a result of their traditional numerical inferiority. As in other plural societies this fear has come to justify itself by creating prejudices about 'the natives', the trepidation being further compounded in Guatemala by the stubborn pride and determination of the Indians not to be incorporated into a Ladino state.

Measuring discrimination is intensely complicated by cultural divisions which are in themselves cemented by discrimination. Health care is one criterion often cited; the discrimination being both economic, with rural — and thus Indian — areas receiving virtually no attention, and cultural in that Indian ways and medical thinking are not considered. Despite their ideal concept of total health, Indians are far from healthy physically. Life expectancy among Indians is 16 years lower than that of Ladinos — 45 years compared to 61.4.[16] Indigenous infant mortality rates may be as high as 134 per 1000 live births compared to a national average of 80, according to Oxfam America, while 82% of children under five suffer from malnutrition to one degree or another.[17] Doctors who regularly examine indigenous children claim that virtually all are anaemic, suffering from parasites and malnurished.

But — true to the government's claim — there are now health posts and medical centres throughout Indian areas. The real problem is an almost total lack of materials and staff combined with the indigenous people's belief that whatever is offered does not meet their needs in any case. In 1987 the Ministry of Public Health received barely 8% of the national budget and even this figure — insufficient to implement the Ministry's basic health plan — was cut a further 10% in 1988.[18] Such cuts helped give Guatemala the world's fifth lowest rate of expenditure on social programmes in relation to income.[19]

Though 61% of the population (overwhelmingly indigenous) lives in rural areas, 80% of the country's health resources are concentrated in Guatemala City.[20] In the countryside there is one doctor for every 23,000 people and the same number of children under the age of five die annually as a result of the lack of primary health care.[21] The three top causes of death in the years 1983-85 illustrate this perfectly: gastrointestinal infections (25.5%), influenza and pneumonia (17.8%), measles (3.9%), are all preventable conditions.[22]

Education provides a similar illustration of the central government's discriminatory integration strategy and resource allocation. Even when schools were available in the locality Indians have often not attended them because from the earliest ages they were needed to help work the *milpa*, wash, weave, or care for younger children. School hours were not matched to their needs; in some secondary schools uniforms were compulsory and Indian dress was not permitted, and — above all — teaching was in Spanish after a first year of 'Castilianization' that could be culturally brutal. Few saw the point of what was taught in the urban-orientated curriculum. As a result a mere 19% of indigenous over seven are literate, compared to nearly 50% of Ladinos, according to Oxfam America.[23]

Economics are the other side of the coin. In most Indian families all resources are channelled toward basic survival and there is no money for the textbooks and pencils schoolchildren require. While 20,000 Guatemalan teachers are unemployed, many rural schools are unstaffed. 'I've got teachers working as servants', complained one Ministry of Education official.

The reality is that real incomes have fallen precipitously in the last decade. In January 1988 the official minimum wage was raised to Quetzal (Q) Q.4.25 (US $1.57) but this was the first such increase for nearly eight years and the buying power of this daily rate remains Q.0.93 lower than that of 1980 as a result of rampant inflation — up to 37% in 1986.[24] In any case, few employers bother to pay the minimum wage as it is not enforced. Most plantation owners were offering Q.3.00-3.20 per day in 1989 if they were hiring at all.[25]

According to the government's own figures, the average family of five needed Q.10.00 per day just to satisfy subsistence needs yet 3.5 million people — about 43% of the total population — were living on less than this in 1988. Most indigenous families are well below this mark, living on an average of Q.3.50-4 per day according to aid workers. The government admitted the urgency of the situation with the launch of its 'Guatemala 2000' long-term economic plan in June 1988, one of whose aims was to get living standards back up to 1980 levels by the turn of the century. Unfortunately the plan itself represented the triumph of neo-liberal economists over those calling for bigger public sector investments in order to pay off the so-called 'social debt'. Indeed, one of the plan's first effects was to lift 'unnecessary' price controls: the cost of beans rose 10% and that of sugar 20% immediately.

But the root of such appalling socio-economic conditions is, of course, land distribution. The GINI coefficient, the accepted method of measuring land distribution, showed that in 1979 — the last year for which comprehensive figures are available — Guatemala had the worst land distribution ratio in Latin America.[26] Two tendencies in land distribution are apparent. Firstly, land is becoming concentrated into bigger units as export-crop agro-industrial mechanization, unrestrained by any form of government intervention, exerts an ever-tightening grip. In 1979, 65.4% of the country's farmed land was part of plots of 45 hectares or more.[27] This was more than double the percentage recorded 15 years previous in 1964.

Secondly, the smallest farms are getting smaller, their overwhelmingly Indian occupants becoming 'subsistence' farmers or landless labourers. In 1950, there were 74,269 plots under 0.7 of a hectare. By 1964, this number had climbed to 85,083 and by 1975 the figure had virtually doubled to 166,732.[28] The acceleration in this trend continued, with the number reaching 250,918 in 1979 when these micro-plots accounted for 41.1% of the country's farms yet only 1.5% of the country's cultivated area.[29]

Indeed, by 1979, 89.8% of Guatemala's farms were smaller than the 7 hectares considered the minimum necessary to support the average-sized rural family.[30] It was estimated that by 1988, at least 98% of indigenous families were landless or did not own sufficient land to support themselves. No wonder then that the Guatemalan Bishop's Conference started their Joint Pastoral Letter 'The Cry for Land' (published February 1988) with: 'The cry for land is without any doubt the loudest, most insistent and most desperate cry to be heard in Guatemala.'

The Spanish colonists' basic formula had been to control labour by controlling land. Expropriation of indigenous land was designed to create a landless Indian work force that, deprived of its livelihood, would have to work on colonial plantations. This basic equation has, thus, become more pronounced since independence. When coffee (still the basis of the Guatemalan economy) was introduced in the late 1870s, it needed both intensive labour to harvest the crop and the higher mountain land onto which the Indians had retreated to escape Spanish and Ladino colonization. Orders were issued by President Justo Barrios requiring magistrates and departmental governors to surrender 'the number of hands to the planters that they asked for'. Vagrancy laws were passed requiring Indians not working on plantations to work 40 days a year on government projects, such as roads and railways. Debt peonage was legalized. Simultaneously, over 100,000 acres of Indian communal land were expropriated on the grounds that they were not being productively employed. Communal lands were simply made illegal.

Expropriation was a cultural attack of the first order. The Indian communal land system — where terrain was divided according to need — was a cornerstone of indigenous society. The law not only forced Indians to own land individually, it obliged them to divide already small plots among all their sons and become the migrant labourers the agro-export-dominated government had always wanted.

Today, as many as 650,000 highland Indians make the annual migration to the coastal plantations. Whole families are transported in open trucks to coffee, cotton or sugar cane *fincas* (plantations). Many are housed in *galeras* (open sleeping barns) where privacy and sanitation were recently described by the International Labour Organization as 'totally unacceptable with regard to hygiene, health, education and morality'.[31] Though conditions have improved considerably on some *fincas*, the best most Indians can hope for is a heavy dose of paternalism. Food is often included in the wage structure and, if not, is bought from the owner or his shop.

Many Indians return home scarcely better off and sickness, both on the *fincas* and on return home, is rampant — highland Indians being particularly susceptible to the malaria of the coast and the pesticides often sprayed from planes while they are working. Once again, official legislation means next to nothing. Work code regulations on dismissal, days off and minimal health care are not enforced and few *fincas* pay the legal minimum wage of 4.25 *quetzales* (dollars) a day.

Today Indians are losing their land to Ladino landowners by only slightly more subtle derivatives of debt peonage and direct expropriation. The lack of adequate credit facilities means that many have to pledge their land as security and often lose it as a result of crop failure or other expenses. The fact that many Indians are either too poor or too ignorant of their rights to go to the provincial capital to pay a lawyer to draw up a land title means that judicial claims on their land by bigger landowners are often upheld. Yet again, there is a government agency and law to rectify the problem. The National Institute of Agrarian Transformation (INTA), in practice, effects no such transformation, being chiefly dedicated to distributing state lands or the one-third of the national territory being opened up by the Northern Transfer Strip road and other highways in the Petén. INTA also grossly overestimates its work. In 1978 the agency boasted the handout of 4962 land titles, covering 41,130 hectares. The real figure, according to a recent study, was 1960 titles covering only 14,549 hectares.[32] Although most of the new acreage was handed out to government officials and military officers, there were attempts to settle Indian and Ladino peasants in cooperatives in three specific colonization areas. The problems, as ever, were both cultural and economic. Land being identity, Indians were reluctant to relocate. 'If you leave Patzún for another area then you're no longer a Patzún Indian', points out one aid worker. Proposals to settle 70,000 families in 10 years were soon scrapped and in 1978, the army attempted to forcibly relocate 12,000 *campesinos* in the area.

Those who did relocate usually found themselves abandoned without the most basic necessities and were often settled on poor limestone soil that was, even in the government's opinion, useless for regular crop production. Disappearances and killings in the area intensified as the land, much of it

suitable for big ranch cattle raising, increased in value. Many Indian settlers became the cheap labour force agro-businesses and construction projects needed. Official attitudes to Indian co-ops in the area — 'a form of communism', in one army officer's words — were perhaps best articulated by Colonel Oliverio Casasola, head of FYDEP, the government department responsible for development of the department of the Petén. 'Of the 2849 immigrants to the Petén, 1903 were Indians and 941 non-Indians, since no matter how much sympathy we may have for the Indian problem, they are not the human contingent the Petén needs to progress.'[33]

The effects of such discrimination have revolved around two quite contrary trends. The first has been for Indians to 'Ladinoize' by dropping dress, language, customs and values as the only passport to full participation in Guatemalan society. The second has been to retreat into Indian society as the only sure defence against this same hostile world. 'Ladinoization' is impossible to quantify. According to Guatemalan government censuses the proportion of indigenous people in the national population has declined from 78% in 1774 to 43% in 1964. 'The general trend is a slow reduction in the Indian population', observes one census official. In proportion maybe, but in numbers no. The number of indigenous people is actually increasing steadily and the figures on the supposed reduction in proportion say nothing about how much of this trend is due to indigenous people passing into Ladino society.

Furthermore, even the proportional figures are probably wrong. Both the census office's methods and criteria are dubious. The decision as to whether or not an individual is an Indian is usually left to poorly-trained Ladino officials and it is predominantly rural Indians who escape the censors. Even the census office admits to a 12% error margin. For all these reasons and others, the proportion of Indians in the Guatemalan population is almost certainly higher than the 38% of the official 1981 census and probably a good deal more than the 47.3% figure put forward by John D. Early in 1980.

'Ladinoization' is however a trend and some of its nature is clear. An Indian usually Ladinoizes after leaving his native community. The speed of the process varies enormously but the individual would normally pass through a stage where he or she might be described as 'modified' or between cultures. In addition, it can be said with certainty that the process is occurring much more rapidly in the east and south of Guatemala than elsewhere. Here, indigenous groups like the Pokoman and Chortí are relatively isolated islands in a sea of Ladinos.

There is one other cause of Ladinoization worth noting — conscription into the army. Although some Indian boys do return to their communities after service, recruitment has to be generally considered the most brutal form of Ladinoization in Guatemala as well as yet another infraction of Indian rights. After being kidnapped in a local *cupo* (grab), indigenous conscripts are brutalized until capable of administering the same treatment themselves. One youth grabbed in Sololá told this writer how, on arrival at the local barracks, one of his group was killed during a beating handed out for being too slow off the army truck. Similar stories abound. 'Basic military training is nothing more than brutalized brainwashing', concluded one foreign doctor who worked in the Guatemalan highlands for 15 years.

More remarkable than the Ladinoization trend, however, has been the indigenous' tendency to cut themselves off from the outside world. It is the ultimate in ironies that Ladino racism has contributed enormously to the preservation of indigenous culture, its insults and discrimination leading Indians to seek refuge in their own, known world.

Indians see Ladinos as *sinverguenza* (without shame) and all dishonourable, exploitative qualities are associated with them. Such feelings are usually hidden, especially from foreigners, but, as one writer noted, in the security of his own home an Indian will often express such sentiments. 'The same man who didn't seem to understand that he was being insulted and laughed at during the day will carry on for half an hour about the uncultured brutes who never learn to keep their mouths shut.'[34]

But this method of cultural protection could work only as long as the culture itself is sufficiently robust. If indigenous society began to fragment, so would the shield it provided. Similarly, racism is only possible if those subjected to it will stand for it. What if some Indians decided they wouldn't?

3. Growing awareness: 1944-76

In October 1944 a Guatemalan university professor returned from exile in Argentina to be elected president. Juan José Arévalo stood on a platform of repealing obligatory labour laws, democratic organization of municipal governments and political plurality. He was a reformist and he heralded the most momentous period of change Guatemala's indigenous people had seen since the conquest.

Under Arévalo, and more particularly his successor, Jacobo Arbenz, national political parties spread to Indian *municipios* (towns) and *aldeas*, a rural labour movement sprang up and, finally in 1952, an agrarian reform law was passed. One hundred thousand families received land, numerous Indians won control of their own *municipios* for the first time and labour organization 'provided the campesino and labourer with a device whereby they could confront the employers directly'.[35] Culturally, the reformists' motives were dubious. The constitution still referred to the 'integration' of the indigenous people, but, by the time Arbenz was overthrown in a right wing coup in 1954 a seed had been sown that the Christian Democrat Party (DCG), founded the following year, and Catholic missioners were to nurture for more than a generation.

Firstly, the church. In the mid-1950s, on the basis of such 'communist' threats as Jacobo Arbenz, Guatemala's Archbishop Monsignor Rossell y Arellano secured government permission to launch *Acción Católica* (Catholic Action), a lay catechist movement designed to re-establish Catholic orthodoxy by wresting control of local religion from the *cofradías* as well as acting as a buttress against revolutionary activity. Highland Guatemala was carved up among foreign missionary orders. Spanish Sacred Heart priests went to El Quiché, American Maryknollers to Huehuetenango, Carmelite Spaniards and Italian Franciscans to Sololá. The 119 foreign clergy in Guatemala in 1944 soared to 434 by July 1966. By 1969 the missionaries boasted an estimated 4100 Catholic Action *catequistas* (catechism teachers) in the three towns of the Ixil area of El Quiché alone.[36] By 1981, over 50% of the adult population of the capital of El Quiché, Santa Cruz, were members of Catholic Action, with an estimated 25 to 30% of the population in the smaller towns being members as well.[37]

Many Catholic Action missionaries won favour and acceptance by showing every respect for indigenous culture. They integrated with indigenous communities by living in the villages and learning their languages. Priests and nuns were already respected figures and Catholic Action was presented more as a correction of previous practices than a significant break with the past. Another factor was escape from the cofradía system and its burdensome financial obligations. Paying for the gallons of *aguardiente* (cane alcohol) that were required for the endless rituals of the cofradía, could break a family economically. One aid worker tells of an Indian who had to sell all his family's 200 *cuerdas* of land to serve a year as cofrade. Suicides on appointment as cofrade were not uncommon. Catholic Action gave many villagers the respectable withdrawal they had been looking for, requiring no expenditure and only a few hours a week.

Being a member of Catholic Action was also much more than religion. Co-op membership, literacy class participation and health education often went hand in hand with the movement in communities where the priest or sister was usually a full community member-agriculturalist, basic doctor and teacher all rolled into one. Finally, Catholic Action offered further educational opportunities at the movement's schools, usually in the nearest provincial town.

As its name suggests, the development of Christian Democracy to some extent mirrored that of Catholic Action and the church in the altiplano. The DCG also started out as an anti-communist 'buttress' looking for 'a third way' between the rapid right-wing fanaticism of the party that legitimized the 1954 coup, the National Democratic Movement (MDN, later MLN) and the communist Guatemalan Workers Party (PGT).[38]

Aided by the defection of a faction of its more recalcitrant anti-communists in 1964, the DCG began to adopt more progressive or developmentalist positions and slowly built up widespread support in indigenous areas. Like Catholic Action, it encouraged subsistence farmers to form cooperatives or Christian-orientated trade unions with funds secured from USAID under Washington's Alliance for Progress programme. The Christian Democrat dominated Federación Campesina de Guatemala (FCG), a peasant union, became an important campaigning focal point.

Both the Christian Democrats and Catholic Action benefited from a new openness to change brought about by basic changes in Indian social structure. Yet again, land was the key. A massive population explosion that saw the number of Guatemalans rise from 2.8 million in 1950 to an estimated 7.5 million in 1981 was inevitably reflected in intense pressure on land — most particularly Indian land. It was no coincidence that the department with the highest proportion of Indian residents became the area with the highest percentage of smallest farms. Apart from having to divide smaller and smaller plots among a greater number of sons, Indians found their land under attack from the commercial farming sector. As land became more valuable and Indian farmers found it harder to make any real living from agriculture, more and more highland plots fell into big landowners' hands. Peasant farms lost 25% of their acreage during the 1970s while the area devoted to export crops swelled a staggering 45%.[39]

Wage labour became more common and, as the 1964 and 1973 censuses show, thousands of Indians became a cheap labour supply for the plantations or burgeoning industries of Quetzaltenango and Guatemala City. Ties to community and culture were almost impossible to preserve but, at the same time, this new group of Indians, with what anthropologists termed a 'low residential continuity', was particularly receptive to new ideas in what was, effectively, a new world.[40] As they worked with almost equally poor Ladinos, racial barriers began to break down. Indians who stayed at home found it essential to diversify into cash crops or develop other paying work. Vegetables were grown and transported and whole villages developed specialized rural industries as something of a small trader entrepreneurial class developed.

Most significantly, the vagrancy laws, which as late as 1935 had decreed that those working less than 1.6 *manzanas* (1 manzana = 1.73 acres) must work 150 days on the plantation, became unnecessary as an annual 30, 60, or 90 day migration to the plantations became vital. Yet even harvest time migrations couldn't solve the real problem. While Guatemala enjoyed economic growth rates averaging 5.5% in the 1960s, and even 7.8% in 1977, the daily wage rate of a rural family averaged 1.15 quetzales in 1975, just over a quarter of the minimum considered necessary to subsist.[41]

In the villages, rural Indians turned increasingly to the DCG and Catholic Action sponsored co-ops as a way out. By the latter half of the 1960s and early 1970s, aid workers from the Peace Corps and USAID were on hand to give the process even more impetus. By 1967 there were 145 agricultural, consumer and credit co-operatives in the country. Within nine years the number had grown to 510, with a membership of 132,000 people and 57% of the total number were located in the Highlands.[42]

Co-ops introduced major changes. First and foremost, they got Indians working together in a communal way that was being increasingly lost. Secondly, they broke down traditional social taboos, such as men and women not being permitted to work together. Perhaps most importantly they taught new skills and techniques. Buying, marketing and farming were nothing less than revolutionized in some villages, the new skills adding to members' sense of their own capabilities.

Increased economic and social contact with the outside world was to a large extent made possible and intensified by the coming of radio and roads. Both took the Indian 'out' into another world, while bringing that same world in. 'When we first came there was nothing', said one aid worker in a village on Lake Atitlán. 'Now, there's a road, four boats and even daily buses to Guatemala City.' In the sixties and seventies the new roads brought a rising tide of tourists and almost every Indian met on the mountain trails was soon carrying a transistor radio.

The effects of this social and economic change are probably best divided into two: the psychological impact on indigenous thinking and the physical appearances that were an illustration of it. It is true to say that increased Ladino contact intensified trends towards Westernization, or, at least, produced an awareness of Indian society and values as part of a much wider world.

The changing perception came from inside Indian mentality as well as the outside world. *Cofradia* service or being a subsistence farmer were clearly no longer definitive criteria for being an Indian now that many who were obviously indigenous, did neither. The psychological perception of being an Indian had to be broadened, along with the perception of the Indian world. In essence, the clearly defined Indian concept of 'role' was being eroded. The Indian concept of 'destiny', a conviction that a person's station in life is pre-ordained and that he/she must remain in the role into which he is born, was disappearing. This amounted to Indians being capable of equality with Ladinos — a concept reinforced by the missionaries basic tenet that all men were equal in the eyes of God. This thinking was further emphasized by the fact that some Indians began to receive secondary education and returned to their villages as teachers and even government officials. They were doing what had always been considered Ladino jobs.

From this sprang the most revolutionary concept of all — Indians had rights. The missionaries further emphasized this, both as a tenet of their religion and as a result of their origin in societies where everyone enjoyed equal rights. How years of subservience and dependency might be changed was illustrated by the religious worker who was told by an Indian mother that her child was sick. 'I told her to take her to the doctor', said the aid worker. 'She replied, "If the doctor will do me the favour of seeing the child". That's the result of centuries of subservience. I explained that the doctor is paid a salary to see her child and now she seems to understand that seeing him is her right.'

All these changes became obvious in village life. Although the outlook of many Indians changed, others clung to the old as the best defence against the new. This represented a break-up in the previous unanimous outlook and caused a vicious fragmentation in once homogenous communities. Some joined co-ops, others did not. Some became traders, others did not. Above all, some joined Catholic Action groups or even became Protestants as evangelical churches moved into the Highlands during the 1970s, while others did not. 'Every community experienced a holy war of sorts between *catequistas* (progressives) and *costumbristas* (traditionalists), violence erupted often.[43] Catholic Action's village *directivas* (councils) challenged the *cofradias* directly for control of fiestas and religious rites and many villages developed dual celebrations. Furthermore, Catholic Action members tended to be young and power in the hands of youth challenged the age-authority structure that had been the basis of indigenous society. A new leadership had emerged but how much of the community they led was another question. As health educators, storekeepers, co-op officials and Catholic Action catechists became the new representatives of power and prestige, villages became hopelessly divided, making them,

Table 2
Land Distribution in Guatemala in 1979

Size of Farm Units (hectares)	Number of Farms	Percentage	Surface (hectares)	Percentage
More than 0.69	250,918	41.1	60,871.1	1.5
0.69 to 6.99	296,654	48.7	608,083.2	14.7
7.00 to 45.00	49,137	8.0	774,974.3	18.4
45.01 to 902.00	13,158	2.1	1,793,618.6	42.7
More than 902.00	477	0.1	955,921.6	22.7
Total	610,344	100.0	4,193,468.8	100.0

Source: Shelton H. Davis and Julie Hodson, *Witness to Political Violence in Guatemala: The Suppression of a Rural Development Movement* (Boston: Oxfam America, 1982), 45.

in turn, even more vulnerable to outside influence. In the mid-seventies one aid researcher identified 37 different power groups in a single village.

One symptom of the changes was dress. Many Indian men dropped their native dress and today there are only about 20 villages where men habitually wear complete traditional dress. The reason was apparently obvious. Men came into contact with Ladinos more often, travelling away from home to work and being exposed to Ladino shops, styles and discrimination in the process. But, just as significant a factor cost. 'It's 40 quetzales for Indian trousers', said one Santa Catarina resident, pointing to his friend's multi-coloured knee-length shorts. 'It's only 10 quetzales for these ordinary cotton ones.' But the trend was not all one way. Many younger Indians began to demonstrate their dual world by wearing western clothes away from the village and Indian dress at home.

A further indication of changing consciousness was an increasing demand for education and health care. 'They're not dumb', said one doctor. 'They don't want to go back to the time when they lost 200 children in a simple whooping cough epidemic.' Rejection of western education began to give way to a pride in being literate. 'I can't read but my children can', boasted an Indian father.

It should be stressed that none of this took place in a political vacuum, the transformation of Catholic Action and the Christian Democrat presence from essentially conservative forces to predominately radical ones in the countryside was the result of external events as well as pressures on the ground. On the religious side, the Second Vatican Council (Vatican II) convened by Pope John XXIII in 1962 to explore the Church's *aggiornamento*, or updating, reached its Latin American conclusion at the continent's own episcopal conference in Medellín, Colombia in 1968.

The Latin American bishops questioned the Church's relationship to the inequitable power structures in the continent, called on the Church to establish decentralized base communities and appealed to believers to make 'a preferential option for the poor'.[44] Values such as freedom of conscience and human rights were endorsed as priorities in a move that was to open the way for the concept of liberation theology.

Few saw what an impact Vatican II would have over the next 20 years but nowhere was the potential greater than amongst the exploited, marginalized indigenous communities of Guatemala. Throughout the 1960s, institutionalized violence grew steadily as the country patented the term *desaparecido* ('to be disappeared').[45] In the 1960s, much of the rural repression was concentrated in the predominately non-Indian departments of Zacapa and Izabal where a guerrilla movement, initially led by two young army officers who deserted in the early 1960s, sprung up.

Between 1966 and 1970, some 10,000 non-combatants were killed in the campaign to wipe out an estimated 350 guerrillas and when the 'Jackal of Zacapa', as the ruthless counterinsurgency chief General Carlos Arana Osorio was known, became President in 1970 the new indigenous leadership – along with unionists, students and intellectuals – was increasingly targeted.[46] By the time of the 1974 elections, the repression, grassroots pressure and the growing economic desperation had forced the PDG into its most radical stance yet, its manifesto decrying 'exploitation, social violence and destitution' and promising agrarian reform, a minimum salary and a big expansion of the public sector as the remedy.[47]

In alliance with two other parties, the PDG chose General Efrain Rios Montt as the presidential candidate that gave the reformist coalition the best chance of having an election victory recognized by the Generals.[48] The alliance was widely recognized to have won the vote but not the count. The army imposed its own candidate General Eugenio Kjell Laugerud as president and the country's last chance to avoid widespread civil conflict had been missed. With hindsight, the 1974 fraud was a watershed for most of the new indigenous leadership. 'The message was that peaceful change would be impossible, options were being exhausted', one *catequista* who survived the consequences recalled.

Many who did not realize it then, were to come to the same conclusion as the 1970s wore on. When the second most powerful earthquake in Latin American history hit the Guatemalan highlands on 4 February 1976, the growing social crisis became acute. Twenty-seven thousand people were killed, 77,000 injured and more than one million left homeless. Virtually all of them were Indians living in the kind of homes least able to withstand the tremor. In Guatemala, even earthquakes were discriminatory, it seemed.

The earthquake rapidly accelerated the processes already affecting indigenous communities. The relief effort brought intensified Ladino contact but most importantly it reinforced the lessons many indigenous communities were already learning about the power of their own organization. In particular, it brought Protestants into the Highlands in unprecedented numbers. Some of these, such as mainstream Baptists and Methodists, were dedicated to community action and 'empowering' their villages like Catholic Action. But others, like the myriad of fundamentalist sects who arrived, were intensely conservative, taught a total acceptance of authority, however repressive, and were to add another layer to the divisions in indigenous societies.

By 1976 political polarization had thrown up two clear sides. On the one hand, there was the radical church, the popular organizations such as co-ops, and the unions, actively backing change or simply initiating measures that were affecting change. On the other side was the military and the traditional landowning elite, refusing to countenance the slightest alteration in the status quo.

It is worth noting that the army had emerged from crushing the insurgents in the east of the country, considerably strengthened. US training, military aid and advice had been a key factor with 2000 Guatemalan army officers trained in US military schools between 1957 and 1972. It was also in the 1960s (according to Michael McClintock in his book *Guatemala: The American Connection*) that US Special Forces advisors helped set up the clandestine Regional Telecommunications Centre that was to be the basis for the death squad structure from 1966 onwards.

Thus by the mid-1970s the military and agro-industrial elite had not only the will but the means to confront the growing social pressure for change. However, on the popular side, increasing numbers of indigenous leaders were realizing that persistent fraud was ruling out the normal means of executing change, i.e. elections. They were also becoming increasingly aware of the ruthlessness of their opponents. Yet incredibly the fear that the killings and kidnappings were designed to engender only served to intimidate popular organizers for short periods, if at all. With each cycle of violence intensifying, many started to go underground. Something had to snap.

4. Indian revolt?: 1976-82

In January 1972, sixteen men crossed the cleared strip of jungle that marks the border between Mexico and

Guatemala. Although survivors of a previous guerrilla front in eastern Guatemala, they had totally discarded the traditional leftist thinking that 'backward' Indians were poor revolutionary material. They viewed the indigenous people as the potential vanguard of the revolution, a mass social base from which they intended to forge a 'prolonged popular war' that would last 'ten, perhaps twenty years'. The group's culturally sensitive approach demanded that they learn as much as they taught. 'With them, we learned how to calculate how a tree would fall, to plant with a digging stick, to orient a house . . .' wrote one guerrilla of their first Ixil contacts in the group's Ixcán jungle base.[49] Without firing a shot the guerrillas studied and learnt for more than three years. Then, in mid-1975, they announced their arrival by killing a rapacious Ixcán landowner. They called themselves the Guerrilla Army of the Poor (*Ejército Guerrillero de los Pobres* – EGP).

The EGP were not alone. In the Sierra Madre mountains of Quetzaltenango, San Marcos and Sololá, ORPA, the Organization of the People in Arms (*Organizacion del Pueblo en Armes*) worked silently among Indians and plantation workers for eight years before declaring themselves in 1979. And in the northern jungles of the Petén and Alta Verapáz, Guatemala's oldest guerrilla group, the FAR (*Fuerzas Armadas Rebeldes* – the Rebel Armed Forces) seemed to be rethinking its attitude towards the Indians. 'We know that it is the Indians, half of the population, who will determine the outcome of the revolution in this country', one of the group's leaders had declared as early as 1967.[50]

But it was the EGP's 'general mobilization' plans, calling for the involvement of whole Indian families, that were to have the most impact on indigenous communities. The group's Local Clandestine Committees, their basic village power unit, had Indians organized into sub- committees responsible for logistics, political education, operations and mobilization. Local Irregular Forces aided regular guerrilla units and were responsible for village self-defence. By the end of 1981, this structure was providing shelter, intelligence and food as well as harassing the army on a district, regional and '*frente*' (front) level throughout much of the western highlands. The widespread social base supported up to 400 *combatientes* (armed fighters) in each frente, and they too were overwhelmingly indigenous. A Mexican editor who spent three months with the EGP in Huehuetenango and El Quiché noted that one guerrilla column was '99% Indians (of the Mam, Jacalteco, Achí, Ixil, Quiché, Kanjobal, Cakchiquel and Chuj groups), of these, 30% are young women less than 18 years of age'.[51]

In February 1982, United States Embassy press handouts in Guatemala estimated that eight out of ten guerrillas were Indians, while the State Department put their strength at 3500 combatants, 10,000 members of Local Irregular Forces and 30,000-60,000 actively organized supporters.

Why? What explains the apparently subservient, politically apathetic Indians' apparent conversion to a radical movement?

The overwhelming reason seems to be protection and self-defence, both individual and cultural, along with the growing realization after 1974 that the electoral path to change was firmly barred. The announcement of the EGP's existence and the February 1976 earthquake had brought army occupations of Indian towns and villages, and kidnappings, murders and 'disappearances' became commonplace as each particular community was occupied. It is impossible to relay the full horror or extent of the excesses but, by as early as February 1977 it was reported that killings had included 68 co-operative leaders in the Ixcán, 40 community leaders in

Chajul, 28 in Cotzal and 32 in Nebaj.[52] Bodies that were located were horribly mutilated, dismembered or sexually abused.

Later, this process broadened to encompass wholesale slaughter in a determination to wipe out any protest. On 29 May 1978 more than 100 Kekchí Indians were killed and 300 wounded when their peaceful protest march to the town plaza in Panzós, Alta Verapáz, was met with bullets from 150 soldiers. On 31 January 1980, 39 people were killed including 23 Quiché Indians when security forces stormed the Spanish Embassy that had been occupied in peaceful protest. The sole survivor among the Indians, Gregorio Yuja Xona, was dragged from his hospital bed the following day, despite terrible burns and a police guard. His tortured body was discovered shortly afterwards.

Attacks on Indian communities or indigenous groups, combined with the elimination of Indian community leaders, convinced many that the government was waging an ethnic genocide, and the history of Indian uprisings in Guatemala indicates that the one time the nation's indigenous people will fight back is when they fear cultural annihilation. In some communities, self-defence mechanisms against the army were already operating by the time the guerrillas first made contact. The Indians' deeply entrenched survival instinct dictated that the guerrillas were the best hope. On an individual level, many simply felt they had no choice. One rural development worker told of a friend who stated that her brother had been killed and that 'she was next. She said she had no other choice; it was either death or join the guerrillas'. Another aid worker spoke of friends discussing joining the guerrillas 'on the grounds that they would be safer with them than at home'.[53] It was for most Indians a pragmatic, not a political, decision.

These feelings were reinforced by the guerrillas themselves. Cultural preservation and individual protection were the constant themes of their village meetings as they took every possible step to identify themselves with indigenous communities. guerrillas used Indian languages, arrived en masse to celebrate Indian fiestas, and even employed the *shaman* to 'work spells on the army', according to one Quiché villager. One EGP informant told how even the local custom of paying for brides was tolerated as long as half went to guerrilla war funds. If most Indians' support was hardly a political conversion, the EGP was hardly a hardline Marxist group.

The cultural identification that led to the guerrillas being widely described as 'our army' was further facilitated by the numerous Indian legends that told how one day 'the foreigners' would be driven from the country. Tales of Tecán Umán, the Quiché king killed fighting the Spaniards, and Tata Lopo and his attempt to establish an independent republic in the highlands, became more current. History informed by the Indian sense of balance dictated that the war having come up from the south must return from the north.[54] The time, it seemed to many, had finally come.

Many of those who became active guerrillas bear out the self-defence/protection motive. They tended to be direct victims of army violence or relatives of the same. Landless, workless and even famililess after an army attack, they had nothing more to lose and without the strong social links of relatives and *milpa*, they joined the swelling ranks of Indians receptive to such new ideas as the guerrillas brought.

There were, however, other recruits and other motives. The new Catholic Action co-operative leadership became firm guerrilla sympathizers as they realized that working for peaceful change was both suicidal and unrealistic and that the rebels' teaching on equality, freedom and community was a logical extension of the missionaries' message. Motivated by a Christian sense of right and a desire to protect and expand their social development programmes, Panzós, the Spanish Embassy attack and, most particularly, the 1974 and 1978 electoral frauds were for this group particular watersheds. As hundreds of catechists and 12 priests were singled out for army bullets, more and more religious people came to the EGP's own conclusion that in Guatemala one could 'not be a Christian and not a revolutionary'.[55] Priests began to speak of the guerrillas as 'counter-violent', *combatientes* attended Bible classes and catechism sessions and sometime in 1980-81 Father Fernando Hoyos, a Spanish Jesuit became the first known priest to pick up a gun and join the EGP.

But the guerrillas were not the only radical opposition mobilizing support during this period. As the recession of the late seventies began to bite, growing numbers of non-rural Indians took leading roles in unions, slumdwellers' committees and community groups. Once again, repression forced these groups to broaden their concept of self-defence and seek closer ties with the armed groups. In November 1977, 300 Mam Indians protested at the closure of the tungsten mine where they worked in San Idelfonso Ixtahuacán by marching to Guatemala City. Their arrival drew 100,000 onto the streets and the government met their demands. In March 1976, delegates from 65 unions formed the National Committee of Trade Union Unity (CNUS) and on May Day 1978, a conglomeration of co-operatives, Christian groups and peasant leagues formed the Peasant Unity Committee (CUC), announcing their arrival in a parade that included the largest Indian turnout the capital city had ever seen.

From the start, the CUC acted as a major back-up to guerrilla forces, aiding harassment of the army, self-defence, and — above all — co-ordinating political education among workers on the plantations. In February 1980, the organization shared its muscle by co-ordinating an unprecedented walkout by 75,000 workers on coffee, sugar and cotton plantations. The results were equally unprecedented — the CUC securing a near 300% rise in the legal minimum wage from 1.12 to 3.20 Quetzales a day.

What did all this add up to? The effects of Indian involvement in both the guerrilla and labour movements might be described as an intensification of consciousness, for they were, in essence, a realization of it. Fighting, striking or protesting alongside Ladinos was at least a tacit recognition by Indians that they had something in common even though a recognition of class divisions as more important than ethnic ones was a long way off in most rural Indians' minds. But the success of both the labour and guerrilla movements did give many Indians a previously unknown sense of their own power.

The result of this changing attitude was yet another group of Indians with yet another outlook to be added to an already severely-fractured indigenous society. For the first time in centuries, a significant number of fighting Indians had emerged. 'We are witnessing a new scene with actors different from the Indian who removes his hat, places it on his chest and humbly asks the *patrón* for a few centavos more.'[56]

This change saw hundreds of thousands of Indians give active or passive support to the guerrillas or labour movements. The depth of involvement depended on the individual's perception of the change but most Indians' political connotation of the struggle stretched only as far as believing the guerrillas or union organizers might improve specific aspects of their lives — e.g. protection from army attacks or improved wages and living conditions. Achieving both of these was demanded by the Indians' will to survive, not by political persuasion. In other words, much Indian support for the guerrillas would last just as long as indigenous communities needed protection and just as long as the armed movement could provide it.

But once again, the external context cannot be ignored. General Romero Lucas García had, as President Laugerud's Defence Minister, succeeded him after the 1978 elections described by the *Washington Post* as 'a fraud so transparent that nobody could expect to get away with it'.[57] Within months, the country's two brightest reform-minded democrats — Alberto Fuentes Mohr, leader of the Social Democrat Party (PSD) and Manuel Colom Argueta of the United Front for the Revolution (FUR) — were gunned down on the streets in broad daylight. Scores of their parties' officials suffered a similar fate. By September 1980 Vice President Dr. Francisco Villagrán Kramar had resigned and fled to Washington where he gave Amnesty International vital information on the government's direction of centralised death squads from an annex of the National Palace.[58]

As corruption became endemic and reached unprecedented levels in the higher echelons of government, the economy began to collapse both because of the scale of corruption and the steep drop in the world prices of Guatemala's main commodity exports — coffee, sugar and cotton. Investment and tourism evaporated as the violence increased and for the last two years of Lucas García's presidency it looked as though the country was slipping into complete anarchy. Under the President's brother, General Benedicto Lucas García, it became obvious the army had no strategy to head off the ever-stronger insurgents other than more and more mass repression.

Indeed, the scale of the slaughter by 1980-81 is difficult to comprehend. San Juan Comalapa, San Juan Ixcoy, Santiago Atitlán, San Mateo Ixtatán, Coya, Cotzal, Patzaj and Panimacac were just a few of the Indian towns and villages from which massacres of 20 or more residents were reported in this period. In April 1981, Oxfam America estimated that 1500 indigenous people had been murdered by death squads or regular army troops in the previous two months in the department of Chimaltenango alone.[59] Church sources put the death toll from government operations at 11,000 in 1981 alone.[60] Most of these were indigenous. In such circumstances it was hardly surprising that the guerrillas could not cope with the surge in potential recruits. By the time of the 1982 election campaign, Guatemala was in a state of virtual civil war.

5. Maya massacre

On 23 March 1982, a group of young officers, disillusioned by the army's poor performance in the war and yet another electoral fraud, surrounded the national palace and demanded General Romeo Lucas García's resignation. José Efraín Ríos Montt, the born-again Christian who took his place, claimed power by 'God's will'. In the next three months 'unknown' gunmen's attacks on centrist politicians and intellectuals in the cities came to a virtual halt and, as 'counter-insurgency' intensified, attention shifted to the guerrillas' real power base, the Indian countryside. Barely a day went by without reports of Indians being hacked to death, bombed, raped, shot and, most commonly, burnt alive in their homes. Between 24 March and the end of July, Amnesty International recorded 68 separate incidents.[61] The Indian surnames listed — Xen, Panjoj, Ajú, Yaqui, to cite just a few — made it clear who the real victims were. Even the

Sites of Army Massacres

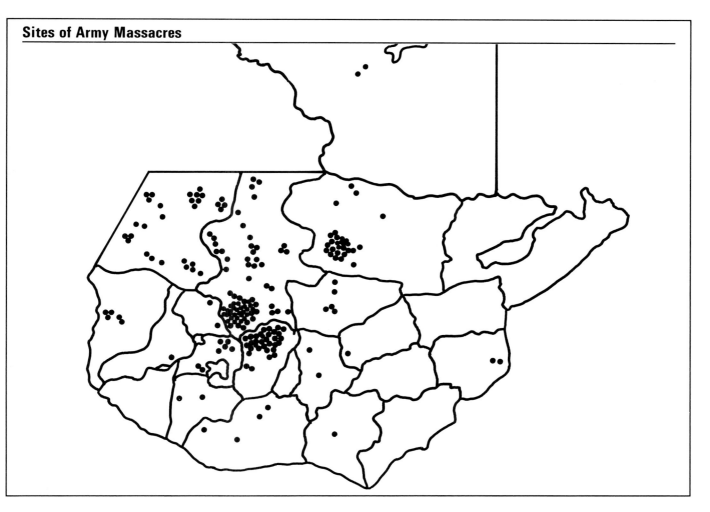

conservative daily paper, *El Grafico*, was moved to an unprecedented outburst. '. . . The type of genocidal annihilation that is taking place in the Indian zones of the country is truly horrifying', stated a May 20 editorial.

But, even this three month butchery was nothing in comparison to what followed. With the press silenced by a ban on independent reports, a 30-day amnesty was followed by the declaration of a 'state of siege', which in Ríos Montt's own words gave the regime 'the juridical framework for killing'. Promising 'a merciless struggle' the General sent 10,000 combat troops into the Indian departments of El Quiché, Huehuetenango, San Marcos, Chimaltenango, Alta and Baja Verapáz and Sololá. Plan Victoria '82 was based on the two-pronged approach put forward by 'The National Plan of Security and Development'. Army sweeps through Indian areas would be backed up by the establishment of a permanent government presence in the form of military garrisons and government development workers. Under the banner '*Fusiles y Frijoles*' (Bullets and Beans) and, later, '*Techo, Trabajo y Tortillas*' (Shelter, work and food) it was a plan of attack that allowed no neutrals. 'If you're with us, we'll feed you; if not, you're dead', one army officer described it.[62]

In essence, the plan was a two-pronged cultural attack on the indigenous people. Not only would they be killed and driven out of their villages, but the development aspect of the plan would bring a massive effort to integrate them into 'national' life. This was what the National Plan meant by 'changes in the basic structure of the state'. But Defence Minister, current President, General Mejía Victores was even more explicit. 'We must get rid of the words 'indigenous' and 'Indian'.

First came the bullets. On the maps in the operation's nervecentre four different coloured pins classified Indian villages according to guerrilla influence. Red meant, in the words of one health worker, in effect 'guerrilla stronghold – wipe everybody out'. Coya, San Miguel Acatán (Huehuetenango), where about 200 Indians were slaughtered on 20 July, and Finca San Francisco, Nentón (Huehuetenango), where more than 300 Chuj Indians were wiped out, were just two of the communities selected for elimination. Amnesty International's October 1982 assessment of 2000 Indians and peasant farmers massacred since the end of the previous March, was described by America's Watch as 'responsible and conservative'. By the next month, the latter group was putting the figure at 10,000.[63]

Although the exact final extent of the devastation in Guatemala during this period will never be known it is worth placing these figures in context. By 1984, the army – which for obvious reasons probably knew best – was saying that 440 villages and hamlets had been destroyed in the counter-insurgency campaign. A study by the Juvenile Division of the Supreme Court in 1984 concluded that at least 100,000 and possible as many as 200,000 altiplano children had lost at least one parent in the violence, leading the lawyers to estimate that at least 50,000 adults had been killed since 1980.[64]

Meanwhile, the Roman Catholic church estimated from its own sources that one million people – out of a highland population of about four million – had been displaced at the height of the violence. Various studies in the altiplano funded by the US Agency for International Development (USAID) came to broadly similar conclusions. Trying to assess the numbers affected by the destruction of homes, displacement and disruption of normal economic activities, these studies concluded that at least 75,000 people in the department of Huehuetenango had been hit; 175,000 in El Quiché; 77,000 residents of San Marcos and Quetzaltenango and 50-80,000 in Chimaltenango.[65]

But the initial 'scientific killing' of Plan Victory '82 had much broader aims than simple elimination. 'Scorched earth' and 'preventive terror' were the military jargon for destructive sweeps through villages marked on the general's maps with pink and yellow pins. Troops shot villagers as they fled, then burned their homes and *milpas*, destroying everything they could find in an attempt to deny the guerrilla's anything that could be of use.

Although some human rights groups have cautiously attributed such incidents to 'armed men', it is worth stating that neither displaced Indians nor the military are under any illusions about who is responsible. Villagers state that they could identify the killers as military because they arrived in the jungle fatigues of the Guatemalan army and often by helicopter. If the culprits were in civilian dress, they noted army boots, haircuts and weapons. Even more condemning is the fact that soldiers talk openly about the nature of the campaign, specifying how they shoot villagers as they flee, then burn their houses and cut down their crops. Some conscripts told this writer that they had been on 'about 80' such operations. Although Indian survivors say that they fled because they were frightened, soldiers maintain that since the villagers were not 'surrendering' they must be guerrillas or be running off to join the guerrillas.

This military attitude that classifies all Indian civilians as guerrillas came right from the top. Ríos Montt's press secretary was quite specific during the 'campaign:' 'The guerrillas won over many Indian collaborators. Therefore, the Indians were subversives. Clearly, you had to kill Indians because they were collaborating with subversion.'[66] Such logic was fed by the campaign itself. Cold and half-starved, those who fled were gradually forced to come out of the mountains and 'surrender' to the army, as if they had been active guerrillas. This, in turn, gave the military a chance to present its acceptable face as well as try and win Indian hearts and minds, as soldiers fed and housed refugees under the 'Beans' part of the campaign.

But emergency relief was only the beginning of a long-term plan designed to control and integrate indigenous communities under the guise of improving their socio-economic condition. The military-run National Reconstruction Committee designated the long-term strategy's stages as 'pre-development' when a basic highland infrastructure would be built up and 'development' when resettled Indians, now grouped in regularly laid-out 'model' villages, 'protected' by army garrisons, would supply the national economy with basic cash crops and labour. As a start, Indians were set to work building roads, reconstructing communities and reforesting mountainsides. The process varied in each locality. In some areas Indians were paid (ironically, less than the legal minimum wage), in others, one day's labour was conscripted free every week or two, and in still others, 'food for work' schemes were developed, with six basic foodstuffs being handed out in fixed quantities.

Nothing illustrated the basic aims of control and integration — not to mention abuse of the indigenous population — better than the formation of Self-Defence Civil Patrols or PACs (*Patrullas de Autodefensa Civil*). All men between the ages of 18 and 60 years (neither age limit seems to apply) are obliged to serve in a civilian militia that both supplements army operations and denies the guerrillas their popular support base. By November 1983, some 700,000 men — nearly one tenth of the population — had been recruited[67] and by mid-1984 the figure was believed to be up to 900,000.

Conditions and demands vary. In the bigger towns, service is often only every 15 days, but in the smallest *aldeas*, it can be every four. While manning checkpoints and patrolling the

bounds of the community are the normal occupations, civil patrols can be called out on active army operations for up to ten days. Unlike the military, many Indians have little food to take, no protective clothing and often little more than rope, machetes or slings as weapons. Families left at home during such extended operations often go hungry until the man returns — if he does. Civil patrollers have, on occasion, been at the forefront of army attacks and just walking the trails are exposed to guerrilla mines and trip-wires. 'Why lose military-trained soldiers when these militias can suffer the casualties?', asked one young lieutenant.[68] The cultural impact of all this was, as it was officially intended to be, devastating. Civil patrols provided the unscrupulous with a means of settling old scores and building up an army-backed power base that allowed them to kill, rape and seize land with impunity.

But, once again, probably the most significant cultural attack was that on land. Incorporation and control the Indian has lived with to some extent for centuries — denied land, indigenous society can erode rapidly as the last generation demonstrates. Because land provided both guerrillas and their indigenous support base with food, as well as providing the Indian with a modicum of independence, military strategists regarded it as the key factor of control in the war. That meant driving tens of thousands of Indians from home and *milpa*, cutting the vital link between location and culture in the process.

Today, thousands of Indians in model villages and refugee settlements cling to minute, postage-stamp size plots of land as the last tenuous link with their former identity as subsistence farmers and thus, to many, Indianness itself. Many families have been split up, undermining the other basic unit of indigenous society. Whatever remains of traditional lifestyle is being worn down by the demands of the army, daily waged labour and what might loosely be termed 'culture shock' as some of the most traditional Indians in Guatemala are integrated into Ladino society — socially, politically and economically.

Despite the force of the odds stacked against them, it is worth noting that the most obvious Indian motivation throughout the whole war has been survival. It was self-preservation that dictated siding with the guerrillas and it is the same instinct that sees most Indians now apparently on the army's side. Survival ordained initial flight from the military and survival later dictated surrender to the same army, as the desperate conditions of refugees coming down from the mountains indicates. An astute ex-guerrilla observed about the indigenous people: 'These people will go with whoever can protect them.'[69]

But, even given the necessity for survival, many Indians do feel they were deserted by the guerrillas, who they claim tended to retreat into the mountains, leaving hopelessly ill-equipped village defence forces to take on helicopters and machine guns. The rationale is simple — to most Indians 'our army' existed to protect them. Despite all the guerrilla promises, few had any conception that the rebels would fail in this, but since they had, they had forfeited their 'raison d'être'.

There are other complaints about the guerrillas, too. In some areas, Indians complain of an increasing number of threats and demands made, bans on alcohol at fiestas and restrictions on travel outside of their villages. This harder line only seems to have emerged in 1981. Although selective guerrilla killings of government *orejas* (informants) or exploitative landlords — usually after warnings — were distinct in indigenous minds, many more traditional Indians found such murders and other examples of guerrilla 'lawlessness', such as pillaging vehicles and farms, too flagrant a violation of their own sense of law and order.

This feeling intensified as guerrilla attacks seemed to broaden during 1981 and 1982 — the killing of civil patrol members being seen as a personal attack on their community and people by many Indians. 'The guerrillas admit they've had to "get tough",' says one Guatemala- based writer. 'I've personally seen Indian bodies left with notes "Submit to the revolution, not the civil patrols".'

Guerrilla attempts to get indigenous communities to work together communally also seem to have caused considerable friction. Any rural development worker in Guatemala will testify how hard it is to get seemingly communally-oriented villages to trust each other sufficiently to pool resources and share workloads. This may be the result of Ladino-imposed values, particularly that of individual rather than communal land ownership, but it is a fact. Guerilla-organized farming co-operatives were generally not liked by Indians and were thus often a failure and counterproductive. 'We'd never been so short of maize as we were that year', an El Quiché refugee complained. 'Nobody worked.'

Ladino-indigenous conflicts seem to be another major reason for guerrilla discredit, particularly among the *combatientes* and those Indians most closely involved. There seems to be widespread disagreement amongst both the rebels and Guatemalan army intelligence officers about what rank Indians rose to in the guerrilla movement. However, it appears that senior commanders were generally Ladinos and foot soldiers generally Indians — a power structure dangerously similar to that on which Guatemala's 450 years of hatred and distrust are based. Conflicts were often deep and bitter. 'We were afraid the Indians wouldn't put their guns down after the revolution', one Ladino ex-guerrilla told a journalist. 'After it's all over, we're going to organize our own revolution', countered one Indian.

Obviously, the major reasons for the erosion of indigenous support for the rebels are military and essentially revolve around the simple fact that the guerrillas could not provide protection when indigenous communities needed it most. But the other reasons given by Indians for not following the guerrillas any more reflect their very non-ideological, individual views of what the guerrillas represent. If the co-operative failed, so had the guerrillas, if they threatened a friend then the rebels, obviously, weren't friendly. And, above all, if they couldn't keep the army out, then what use were they?

6. Reshaping Mayan Society

On 8 August 1983, General Ríos Montt was overthrown in a coup led by his Defence Minister, Brigadier General Oscar Humberto Mejía Víctores. All the new government's aims were characterized by a common thread — stabilization and consolidation. In the countryside this meant eradicating the remnants of subversion while consolidating social control and simultaneously counteracting Guatemala's international pariah image to garner foreign aid to pay for these programmes.

In its own strategic terms, the Mejía Víctores government was brilliantly successful. By the time it handed over power to a nominally civilian government headed by Vinicio Cerezo in January 1986, the army was entrenched in the countryside and in many respects had moved itself onto an equal political footing to that of the business elite that it had traditionally served. Military strategists had developed and implemented a programme in which counter-insurgency and security coincided almost completely with 'development',

establishing what two analysts were later to term 'a state of permanent counter-insurgency in Guatemala'.[70]

Equally crucially, by 1985, dwindling numbers of guerrillas had been pushed right back to the remotest mountains and forest. Denied access to much of their support network, the army seemed to have the EGP in particular, where it wanted them: enough of a threat to justify the massive militarization of the countryside and bloated levels of defence spending, yet no real menace to the new pseudo-democratic state they were forging.

The names of the military's annual programmes — *Firmness '83, Institutional Re-encounter '84, National Security '85, National Consolidation '86* — demonstrate how the aims of the five-year plan begun with Ríos Montt's Victory '82 were institutionalized. But the Orwellian terminology that applied to the Mayan peoples was unmistakable to anyone who took a closer look: 'food for work' = forced labour, 'search and rescue' = hunt and capture, 'secure and protect' = neutralize and imprison.

The basis of the army's strategy were six poles of development, best defined as high security areas where army bases, air strips and artillery were based. The army's own propaganda was quite specific, defining a pole as 'an organized population centre . . . that guarantees the adherence of the populace and their support and participation with the Armed Institution against communist subversion'.[71] Therein lies the nub of the issue: all six poles were located in what had been considered guerrilla strongholds, where, by implication, in the army's view, the population was subversive.

From these poles of development, more than 30 model villages began to radiate, the first, Acul, near Nebaj in the Ixil Triangle (the three Ixil towns of Nebaj, Chajul, and Cotzal) being inaugurated in December 1983. These poles and model villages did, and still do, vary enormously. By 1989, there were 19 model villages in the Ixil Triangle with a further 12 under construction. However, in the Chacaj and Senahú poles there is just one model village in each. Tactical flexibility has been the army's watchword with at least 500,000 living within the scope of the poles of development, although only 10-15% of this total actually live in new model villages.

Conditions in the model villages also vary widely. In some locations, the population is relatively free despite a full-time army presence. However, relaxed regimes tend to be designed for international scrutiny and are located in places where greater control is deemed superfluous. 'Where barbed wire and an overt army presence are no longer necessary, fear and mistrust of one's neighbours provide sufficient control over indigenous movements', one report put it.[72]

In most model villages, particularly Playa Grande in the Ixcán and the Ixil Triangle again, onerous civil patrolling, checkpoints, permission to come and go, barbed wire fences and army watchtowers are the norm. Such features led the Argentine Nobel Peace Price Laureate, Adolfo Pérez Esquivel, to describe the villages as 'concentration camps'. Americas Watch termed the indigenous groups suffering in them 'a nation of prisoners'.

This physical reshaping of the altiplano landscape and the subjugation of the indigenous people and culture located there could only take place in the wake of the army's 1982-83 destruction. Most of those housed in model villages were the survivors of the onslaught targetted at key villages, so in the army's mind were those that had had closest contact with the guerrillas. Some were rounded up immediately, but others spent months and years in the mountains and tropical forest of the remotest part of the country. The 'surrender' of these 'communities in resistance' as they became known was a very gradual process and army operations designed to bomb or starve them out continue to this day.

Yet all this required army infrastructure. Between 1982-85, the number of military zones increased from nine to 22, with all departments now co-extensive with military zones. At the same time, the army launched the Inter-Institutional Coordinator System (IICS) which gave each departmental military zone total jurisdiction over the rural development projects of both governmental and outside organizations. Indeed, public sector organizations were subordinate to the IICS's departmental councils — on which the military commander served as president and the civil commander as vice-president — being required to participate in programmes that the Councils set as priorities. Yet even the civil commanders (commandante civil) and mayors in local communities tended to be appointed by the local military commanders, who also abolished the position of regidor (councilman) who traditionally enjoyed an important role in consensus community rule. Thus by 1984, Indian civil authorities had become virtually defunct.

From October 1983 to November 1984 the IICS applied to only the highland regions but by 1985 the system had been extended to the whole country. It went hand in hand with the creation of S-5, the army's Division of Civilian Affairs and Community Development (CACD) and the expansion of S-2, the military's rural intelligence network. All this was crucial for the maintenance of military power, particularly in the countryside, after President Cerezo took power. Indeed, many senior hardliners in the army would not have acceded to plans for free elections without such infrastructure in place.

The National Reconstruction Committee (CRN) — run by Colonel Eduardo Wohlers Rivas — was the key institution in terms of the implementation of development pole activities. Originally founded after the 1976 earthquake, it received a new lease of life between 1983-86, although it was always nominally subservient to S-5. This, and the fact that all national and international private voluntary organizations became formally responsible to a CRN department, meant that all the commodities donated to the relief effort were effectively requisitioned for what one Guatemalan bishop termed 'the army's own project'.

The 'project' was, however, much more complex and long-term than simply the control of key sectors of the indigenous population and victory in the war against the guerrillas. The army, as we have already seen, planned 'changes in the basic structures of the state', i.e. incorporation of the country's indigenous peoples into what military jargon was now terming 'a strong state' — shorthand for an apparent contradiction in terms, a more powerful military in an army-sponsored democracy.

There was an almost missionary zeal about this end. Addressing the first graduating class of the Army's new School of Ideological Warfare in June 1984, Colonel Marco Antonio Sánchez explained how to 'fight and defeat the enemy in the terrain of ideas' with a forceful projection of an 'authentic Guatemalan nationalism'.[73]

'The existence of 23 ethnic groups demonstrates that we are not integrated; we lack a national identity. Who better than the men in uniform to project ourselves to every last corner of the Fatherland bearing the message of nationalism.'[74] With such remarks, notice was formally served that the country's indigenous people, having already suffered the most vicious

physical assault since the Spanish conquest, were to be subjected to a cultural onslaught, the aim of which was nothing less than their elimination as separate ethnic entities.

Re-education followed re-location from late 1983. The basis for this were the ideological talks at the ad hoc refugee camps that housed the displaced before they could be set to work building their own model villages, or the specialist re-education camps such as Nuevo Acamal near Cobán, Alta Verapaz. In what human rights groups described as brainwashing sessions, indigenous people were submitted to ideological talks, civil defence training and lectures on patriotic symbols.

The simplest aspects of these regimes such as flag raising and lowering to the singing of the national anthem, found their way into all the model villages as 'official' celebrations such as Army Day and Independence Day took the place of traditional indigenous fiestas. 'It's like rewinding a cassette, because this is like a tape recording and you have to keep taping it over again and again', concluded the sergeant in charge of re-education at the Tzacol refugee camp.[75] 'Indians are very susceptible; they are easy to ply, just like clay', concluded Major Saúl Figueroa Veliz, head of S-2 in Cobán.[76]

The cultural abuses inherent in this process were horrific. Families and communities already split and traumatized were often resettled away from their most important identification symbol, their land. The mixing of different linguistic groups meant that Spanish had to become the lingua franca in many model villages. Meanwhile, those that were within walking distance of their milpas were often prevented from working on them, by a military keen to develop Indian dependence and to prevent any possibility of supplies falling into guerrilla hands.

Those that did continue farming, albeit often on others' land allocated by the army — another means of dividing and undermining indigenous society — were encouraged or even forced to grow cash crops, thus breaking the traditional link with maize. The model villages themselves — regularly laid out wood and corrugated tin huts dissected by broad avenues which could double up as landing strips in an emergency — were a cultural shock to most indigenous people. They could not have contrasted more sharply with the sprawling hamlets which were the basic Mayan settlement pattern.

Throughout the 1983-86 period abductions and killings continued and there were plausible reports of less frequent massacres in those parts of the country that remained zones of conflict. However, the general pattern in both the development poles and the remainder of the altiplano was selective assassination, often carried out as a result of army pressure on civil patrols. By 1984, the patrols were undoubtedly the military's single most important vehicle for both securing the population and undermining indigenous society by means of disrupting the age-grade structure, economic activity and encouraging individuals to inform on each other.

Jean-Marie Simon cites one typical incident whereby the army presented five villagers to the local civil patrol, told them they were guerrillas and asked them to decide what to do with them. Despite knowing that the accused were innocent, the village took a community decision to kill the five in order to save the rest of the village from a possible massacre. After asking their forgiveness, the patrollers shot the five only to find the soldiers, who had been hidden nearby, on the scene within minutes.[77] Such instances of PAC members having to choose between killing or being killed were common. As one civil patroller from Patzún told Americas Watch: 'This is what hell must be like.'[78]

The economic consequences of all this political upheaval were devastating and probably represented as great a long-term threat to indigenous society as the physical abuses themselves. With the productive capacity of the highlands crippled by depopulation, forced labour, civil patrolling and the general disruption of normal trading patterns, malnutrition and related health problems became more common. Prices were forced up as a result of shortages, but many were not allowed by the army to follow the traditional migration patterns to the coastal plantations to boost family income. Equally significantly for many families and their womenfolk who often sold pieces of weaving, tourism dried up.

In some ways, the economic crisis reflected that affecting Guatemalan society as a whole in the 1983-86 period. Inflation increased nearly sixfold to 18.7% in 1985, then doubled again to 37% in 1986, while the minimum wage, if paid, remained fixed. GDP growth per capita shrunk steadily and dramatically throughout the mid-1980s and a growing foreign exchange crisis was reflected in the devaluation of the quetzal. Indigenous communities, at the bottom of the economic pile, disrupted by war and under military rule, were least able to protect themselves.

The army counteracted such criticism with elaborate press briefings on the merits of their 'development' projects for the highlands. They pointed to health posts, schools, running water, electricity and roads in their model villages. 'These people have been neglected for centuries, that's how the guerrillas won them over in the first place', one army captain told this writer in 1984. 'We have to improve things up here.'[79]

'Improving things' was indeed the 'hearts and minds' of the military's overall project, but such an aim was never more than a distant second to security and counter-insurgency concerns. While schools and health centres have been built in the model villages most often shown to visitors, drugs, books and staff are almost non-existent. Moreover, many model villages remain totally bereft of facilities and resources, while the scores of communities that have returned to reconstruct their own villages are even more evidently worse off than before the violence.

Yet the most important issue remains the appropriateness of the development now foisted on indigenous communities and the terms on which it has been made available. 'You have roads, but how many Indians have cars?' asked one development expert. 'What use is electricity if you have no means of earning to pay for it.'

The truth, of course, was that any 'development' proffered during this period was on the army's terms, with no indigenous consultation whatsoever. Roads were designed to enable army trucks and jeeps to travel, rather than Indians. Electricity and telecommunications posts were for military communication, not for Mayans. Indeed, by 1986 even the army-inspired construction programme had been stagnant for more than a year as the funds dried up. Only one new model village was inaugurated in 1986, the year the new civilian President Vincio Cerezo took power, as it became obvious that thousands of impoverished and displaced Mayan Indians were to be left in limbo in holding camps for the foreseeable future.

7. All change but no change

President Vinicio Cerezo — the first civilian the army had allowed to take power for 16 years — was inaugurated President in January 1986. The 41-year old Christian Democrat's accession seemed to be considered a positive step only by outside observers and then only in relation to the desperation of the country's immediate past. Few Guatemalans had any illusions about how much power the new President would wield. Indeed, the election campaign was noticeable for its complete avoidance of the real issues — human rights, land reform and the army's 'development' of the countryside seemed to be taboo issues.

The image rather than any substance was the message; elections were an end in themselves, for the poll meant Guatemala was now 'democratic' and as such eligible for significant foreign aid and a platform in international forums. Although there had been no overt deal with the military before his accession as in other Latin American states going through the same process, Cerezo knew where he stood. Asked if there would be trials for human rights abuses, the new President replied: 'We are not going to be able to investigate the past. We would have to put the entire army in jail.'[80]

The military also knew where they stood. Days before Cerezo took power they decreed an amnesty forbidding any prosecutions of military personnel for actions carried out 'in the course of their duties'. The arrogance was epitomized by Mejía Victores' press officer, Colonel Edgar D'Jalma Domínguez, when asked about the possibility of military trials: 'Do you think we've left proof?' he retorted. 'In Argentina there are witnesses, there are books, there are films . . Here in Guatemala there is none of that. There are no survivors.'[81]

The comparison carried a subliminal significance for the Guatemalan military's arrogance was largely inspired by their belief that they had vacated the National Palace as victors in their war against the guerrillas, not defeated like the Argentines had been in the Falklands/ Malvinas. Democratization in fact strengthened the army, preventing the military from having to take the flak for the economic crisis while boosting aid flows for their 'development' project. Civilian political parties would and do fight each other, not the military. D'Jalma himself said shortly after Cerezo took power: 'For convenience sake a civilian government is preferable . . the real power will not be lost.'[82]

It soon became obvious that the basis of the army's power, its control of the countryside, was to remain intact, leaving the country's indigenous people the real victims of the tacit deal between the new government and the military. Just one month after being sworn in as President, Cerezo confirmed his approval of the model villages by inaugurating the Chisec development pole in Alta Verapaz. He even claimed that the poles had been part of the Christian Democrat's programme since the 1960s. Meanwhile, the new Minister of Development René de León Schlotter stated quite categorically that the main purpose of his ministry was 'to combat subversion ideologically, in much the same way as the army had been doing through the IICs'.[83]

President Cerezo had always maintained that the key issue was who controlled the rural programmes and in this respect there were a few changes, albeit as superficial as the nature of the democracy itself. The IICs were formally replaced by Councils of Development and their military leaders substituted by 22 civilian governors although on the ground both projects and the model villages remained as tightly controlled by the military as ever. Civil Defence Patrols were renamed Voluntary Civil Defence Committees, with President Cerezo making a great show of the fact that patrolling was not now mandatory. The reality was that in the areas where the military considered them strategically important the patrols were just as compulsory as before.

Above all the human rights abuses continued, with G-2, the army intelligence division, highlighted as the hub of what

Amnesty International had described as a government programme of political murder, 'more comfortably entrenched than at any time since the mid-1960s'.[84] The numbers of killings and kidnappings did actually fall, although this was relative, the lowest figures recorded by the various human rights groups in 1986 being 132 disappearances and 268 political murders. The structures responsible for the human rights abuses remained in place. Indeed, with the massive militarization of the countryside they had been reinforced. This became self-evident in 1987 and 1988 when all the human rights' groups monitoring the situation agreed that there had been significant increase in killings and disappearances.

It was this failure of the new democracy to bring any significant improvements that saw indigenous people becoming actively involved in several pressure groups that sprung up. The first and most vociferous of these was the Mutual Support Group or GAM. Founded in 1984 by five women who had met each other in city morgues looking for the bodies of husbands and sons who had disappeared, it grew rapidly. By 1986 it had more than 1000 members, 850 of them Indian and nearly all women.[85]

The GAM's incredible success in keeping the issue of the disappeared high on the political agenda was largely due to the courage of its leadership and general membership. Weekly demonstrations outside the National Palace were an unprecedented step for any opposition group in Guatemala, let alone an organization composed largely of the most marginalized sector of Guatemalan society, indigenous women. A reaction was inevitable and over Easter Week in 1985 two of the group's leaders, Hector Gómez Calito and Rosario Godoy de Cuevas were tortured and murdered, along with Rosario's 21-year old brother and two-year-old son.

But GAM's demands for information on the fate of the disappeared continued and under Nineth Montenegro de García the group began to present evidence of military responsibility and widen their demands to include social and economic rights. For perhaps the first time in Guatemalan history, indigenous and ladina women worked side-by-side in a common cause and hundreds of widows from the highlands learnt how to organize and protest. 'Above all we learnt we were not alone in our suffering and a great strength that I never knew I had came from that', one GAM member told this writer in 1986.[86]

GAM was followed by the formation in 1988 of the Council of Ethnic Communities *Runujel Junam* (meaning 'everyone is equal' in Quiché) or CERJ in Santa Cruz del Quiché, the capital of El Quiché. CERJ's declared aim is to pressure the Guatemalan government to respect human rights and to struggle 'to advance the goals of democracy, justice and dignity for the Mayan peoples while fighting racial discrimination'.[87] Like GAM, CERJ under the leadership of Amílcar Méndez Urízar is dedicated to non-violence and concentrates on the enforcement of constitutional rights as they apply to indigenous people. Articles 66-70, which address the cultural and ethnic rights of Mayan peoples, and Article 34 which prohibits the forced participation in civil defence patrols, have been the main campaigning points to date as the group has expanded by setting up branch offices in Totonicapán and Sololá.

Indigenous people also played significant roles in other popular organizations. The National Coordinating Committee of Guatemalan Widows (CONAVIGUA), established in 1988 included many Mayan women as it made broad demands for material support for families of victims of violence. Many indigenous people were also organized for

the first time as part of UNISITRAGUA, an independent labour federation that brought together more than 40 unions in the industrial, agricultural and service sectors. In 1988, the CUC emerged from underground to ally itself with a broad spectrum of popular organizations in the UASP, the Unity of Labour and Popular Action. One indication of the CUC's growing strength was a January 1989 strike call that saw up to 70,000 agricultural workers on coffee, sugar and cotton plantations strike for higher wages.

Yet the most significant development on the land issue during this period was the formation of the National Association of Peasants for Land (ANC) under Father Andrés Girón. Within months of Cerezo's inauguration, Girón led 16,000 *campesinos* from his parish in Nuevo Concepción in Escuintla on the south coast in a 'March for Land' to the National Palace in Guatemala City. The idea was to test the government's commitment to making land available for purchase and Girón, although claiming that wholesale land reform was the only answer to the country's problems in the long term, was initially keen to stress that the ANC wanted to purchase land on concessionary terms and secure credit to work it collectively.

By 1989, the ANC had more than 150,000 members, and some groups, tired of token moves by the Cerezo administration, had taken to 'invading' fallow land. By 1988 the President had been forced to distribute five farms to peasant groups like the ANC thanks, in part, to a US $8.4m donation from the European Community that allowed the purchase of 7700 hectares. Girón had lit a torch, condemning INTA as 'an evil organization created for the very purpose of making all land reform a failure'.[88]

The dynamic priest was soon credited with sparking the development of an open private land market, something that had never existed before in Guatemala. Coming from the coastal region most of Girón's followers were poor, landless Ladinos rather than Indians, although by 1988-89 land invasions were taking place in predominately Indian departments like San Marcos. However, the ANC followed the pattern set by the other popular pressure groups with or without predominately Indian memberships — they were all led, like the EGP, by Ladinos. On the political scene, at least, the beginnings of a Mayan leadership seemed to be emerging.

In the July 1984 constituent assembly elections there had been clear signs that an Indian political consciousness had been awoken by the violence. Two Quiché Indians and one Cakchiquel won seats for the departments of Totonicapán, El Quiché and Chimaltenango on the Christian Democrat slate in that election. However, the most surprising victory was that of Mauricio Quintán who claimed one of Quetzaltenango's four seats running for the indigenous Peasant Social Action Organization, the first representative of an all-Indian party to be elected to national office in Guatemala. Although some cast doubt on the validity of Quintán's indigenous credentials, it was an undoubted breakthrough and all four deputies worked hard to push indigenous issues up the political agenda.

8. Refugees and the international dimension

One of the biggest indigenous issues under the Cerezo government has been the refugees. Once again it is a matter of appearance as much as substance, the government finding it difficult to maintain that it is developing a flourishing democracy or that the civil strife in Guatemala is over while tens of thousands of nationals remain in exile, fearing for their lives.

It is impossible to say how many fled Guatemala at the height of the repression but it seems certain that at least 200,000 — the vast majority indigenous — made it over the border to Mexico. Some of these went onto the United States while several thousand more sought refuge in Honduras and Belize. The extent of the diaspora could be measured by the swollen Guatemalan communities in Mexico City, Los Angeles and even Canada. One of the most interesting from an anthropological perspective was the several hundred Kanjobal Mayans who settled as a community in Indiantown, Florida, a migrant community where work and asylum petition facilities were readily available.[89]

Stimulated by the Esquipulas peace process, the government's Committee for Aid to Returnees (CEAR) has enjoyed some success in persuading exiles to return. According to CEAR's own figures, some 13,500 Guatemalans had returned spontaneously or under the auspices of the United Nations High Commissioner for Refugees (UNHCR) by December 1988.[90] However, the problems of effective guarantees of treatment — in essence the fact that the Cerezo administration's writ does not run in army-controlled rural areas — remains the major obstacle. 'People don't trust them at all — would you?' asked one priest at a refugee camp in Chiapas, Mexico in 1986. 'Returnees are regarded with particular suspicion by the army. To their mind these are the ones that got away.'[91]

For many indigenous communities, exile was almost as traumatic as the massacres and repression that had provoked it. Uprooted from their ancestral lands around which individual ethno-linguistic villages revolved, many found their identity evaporating. During 1982-85, Guatemalan army raids over the border into Chiapas were common and for many the trauma was intensified when the Mexican government began a relocation scheme which saw the construction of four major camps in Campeche and Quintana Roo, hundreds of miles away from the frontier. This, to many refugees, seemed to rule out the possibility of a quick return and in many cases took them away from their cultural cousins in Mexican Mayan communities.

There has undoubtedly been a more rapid loss of indigenous identity in the Campeche and Quintana Roo camps than in those in Chiapas, although this is due to structure and development as much as location. The four camps to the north of Chiapas are larger, ranging in size from 1600 to 7500 inhabitants, are regularly laid out and have been considerably organized by the refugees themselves as well as COMAR, the Mexican agency dealing with them. A Permanent Commission of about 60 representatives from all the camps including the 26 smaller ones in Chiapas meets regularly and has now set out five conditions that must be met by the Guatemalan government before any mass return.

'We want to go home but under the current circumstances it's impossible', Lucas Lima Díaz, one of the Permanent Commission representatives from Quetzal-Edzná camp in Campeche, told this writer in January 1989. Leaders at the camp agreed that the loss of Mayan culture 'particularly among our children' was the biggest problem.[92] Although individual villages and linguistic groups have been congregated together in the same streets and barrios, COMAR's relaxation of a ban on work outside the camp means that young men and women are travelling as far as the Mexican holiday resorts of Cancún to work on construction sites or in hotels. Make-up and English motif T-shirts are now common; indigenous *trajes* are not.

The refugee exodus did, however, serve to focus the international spotlight on what was going on in Guatemala. Although the war and massacres remained a sideshow in media terms compared to the coverage afforded the wars in El Salvador and Nicaragua, Guatemalan voices were increasingly heard in international forums from 1983 onwards. The leading human rights groups, Americas Watch and Amnesty International, stepped up efforts with more reports and lobbying while refugees helped by the Sanctuary Movement, which offered refuge in homes and churches in North America, began to attract media attention with their testimonies.

A major catalyst from the indigenous perspective was the publication of 'I . . . Rigoberta Menchú' in 1984. It was hard to quibble with the publisher's description of the text as 'one of the few complete expressions of Indian self-knowledge since the Spanish conquest'. Ms. Menchú, a Quiché Indian who became a CUC leader after the murder of her brother, father and mother in separate incidents of army brutality, simply told her story in what *The Times* of London described as 'a fascinating description of the culture of an entire people'. However, the most important message as Rigoberta says in her first few lines is that: 'My personal experience is the reality of a whole people.' By 1988 the book had run into seven editions.[93]

From 1982, indigenous peoples were able to present cases at a special United Nations working group established the previous year. Mayan groups were among the first to avail themselves of this opportunity and in August 1988 the United Indian Delegation of Guatemala represented by Gabriel Ixmatá of the Guatemala Cooperative Movement (MCG), Francisco Calí of the Highlands Campesino Committee (CCDA) and Rigoberta Menchú and Rosario Pu of the CUC, made the most complete presentation to date. At that session, the working group established a draft Universal Declaration on Indigenous Rights as the first step on the long road to the adoption of a United Nations Convention.[94] (see page 26 for text)

Table 3
Location of Guatemalan Refugees/Displaced Persons

Location	Number
State of Campeche, Mexico	12,300
of which (settlements):	
Quetzal Edzná	4,800
Maya Tecun	7,500
State of Quintan Roo, Mexico	6,000
of which (settlements):	
Los Lirios	1,600
Maya Balam	4,400
State of Chiapas	75,000
of which:	
In refugee camps	55,000
Not in refugee camps	20,000
In other parts of Mexico	50,000
In other countries	50,000
Internal refugees within Guatemala	500,000

Source: UNHCR

However, there were setbacks. After determined lobbying by the Guatemalan government, the General Assembly of the United Nations decided in February 1987 to mark an 'improvement' in the human rights situation in Guatemala

UNITED NATIONS
DRAFT DECLARATION OF PRINCIPLES FOR INDIGENOUS RIGHTS

1. Indigenous nations and people have, in common with all humanity, the right to life, and to freedom from oppression, discrimination and aggression.

2. All indigenous nations and peoples have the right to self-determination, by virtue of which they have the right to whatever degree of autonomy or self-government they choose. This includes the right to freely determine their political status, freely pursue their own economic, social, religious and cultural development, and determine their own membership and/or citizenship, without external interference.

3. No State shall assert any jurisdiction over an indigenous nation or people, or its territory, except in accordance with the freely expressed wishes of the nation or people concerned.

4. Indigenous nations and peoples are entitled to the permanent control and enjoyment of their aboriginal ancestral-historical territories. This includes surface and subsurface rights, inland and coastal waters, renewable and non-renewable resources, and the economies based on these resources.

5. Rights to share and use land, subject to the underlying and inalienable title of the indigenous nation or people, may be granted by their free and informed consent, as evidence in a valid treaty or agreement.

6. Discovery, conquest, settlement on a theory of *terra nullius* and unilateral legislation are never legitimate bases for States to claim or retain the territories of indigenous nations or peoples.

7. In cases where lands taken in violation of these principles have already been settled, the indigenous nation or people concerned is entitled to immediate restitution, including compensation for the loss of use, without extinction of original title. Indigenous peoples' desire to regain possession and control of sacred sites must always be respected.

8. No State shall participate financially or militarily in the involuntary displacement of indigenous populations, or in the subsequent economic exploitation or military use of their territory.

9. The laws and customs of indigenous nations and peoples must be recognized by States' legislative, administrative and judicial institutions and, in case of conflicts with State laws, shall take precedence.

10. No State shall deny an indigenous nation, community, or people residing within its borders the right to participate in the life of the State in whatever manner and to whatever degree they may choose. This includes the right to participate in other forms of collective actions and expression.

11. Indigenous nations and peoples continue to own and control their material culture, including archeological, historical and sacred sites, artifacts, designs, knowledge, and works of art. They have the right to regain items of major cultural significance and, in all cases, to the return of the human remains of their ancestors for burial in accordance with their traditions.

12. Indigenous nations and peoples have the right to be educated and conduct business with States in their own languages, and to establish their own educational institutions.

13. No technical, scientific or social investigations, including archeological excavations, shall take place in relation to indigenous nations or peoples, or their lands, without their prior authorization, and their continuing ownership and control.

14. The religious practices of indigenous nations and peoples shall be fully respected and protected by the laws of States and by international law. Indigenous nations and peoples shall always enjoy unrestricted access to, and enjoyment of sacred sites in accordance with their own laws and customs, including the right of privacy.

15. Indigenous nations and peoples are subjects of international law.

16. Treaties and other agreements freely made with indigenous nations or peoples shall be recognized and applied in the same manner and according to the same international laws and principles as treaties and agreements entered into with other States.

17. Disputes regarding the jurisdiction, territories and institutions of an indigenous nation or people are a proper concern of international law, and must be resolved by mutual agreement or valid treaty.

18. Indigenous nations and peoples may engage in self-defense against State actions in conflict with their right to self-determination.

19. Indigenous nations and peoples have the right freely to travel, and to maintain economic, social, cultural and religious relations with each other across State borders.

20. In addition to these rights, indigenous nations and peoples are entitled to the enjoyment of all the human rights and fundamental freedoms enumerated in the International Bill of Rights and other United Nations instruments. In no circumstances shall they be subjected to adverse discrimination.

by downgrading its concern. Hector Gros Espiell, an Uruguayan, was appointed as a UN 'special expert' to simply make recommendations to the General Assembly in the place of a 'special rapporteur'. The latter represented the highest level of UN concern, having to make regular trips to Guatemala and present full reports to the General Assembly.

Many argued that the end of Lord Viscount Colville of Culross's mandate as a special rapporteur on Guatemala was in fact no loss. The British peer was heavily criticized by a number of human rights groups for unilaterally redefining his mandate, his naïveté in using the army as his main channel of inquiry and for constructing his reports on the basis of his own political agenda for Guatemala.[95] 'How do you persuade a military government to give up its power and go back to the barracks? You don't do that by writing a 100-page report of pure condemnation', he told the *Wall Street Journal*.[96]

9. Now and forever

Anyone who doubts that the processes begun in 1982 or, perhaps more pertinently, 1521, are continuing today need only take a trip to the Guatemalan highlands or read the specialist press covering the country. At the end of 1987 the army launched an 'End of the Year Offensive' which continued well into 1988. According to the Guatemalan Church in Exile and reporters who visited the areas concerned, the campaign has killed scores of Indians, displaced about 7000 more and forced a further 3000 refugees hiding in the mountains and forests to 'surrender' to the military.[97]

The army has revealed plans to set up 17 more model villages in the Ixil triangle alone, part of a new scheme labelled 'Development and Peace Projects of the Ixil and Ixcán' that was supposed to follow victory in the End of the Year Offensive. The war and counter-insurgency campaign disguised as development go on and, apparently, could do so indefinitely. The price of all this is, of course, the loss of Indian culture, as the military always intended it would be.

Drawing general conclusions is difficult but important. Summarizing her research based on the highland municipality of San Mateo Ixtatán, the Ixil region of El Quiché and the northern lowland area of Ixcán, the anthropologist Beatriz Manz reached three broad conclusions: 'The military has embedded itself in the countryside in new and far-reaching ways, forcing major cultural adaptations; political constraints continue to prevent fundamental economic and social reform and the essential guarantees of life and safety are absent.'[98] This writer believes that such conclusions could be applied to virtually all Mayan communities as a result of events in the last decade. The difference between individual villages is purely a matter of degree.

The mass terror of the early 1980s and its sequel, counter-insurgency and social control disguised as development, was initially provoked by an armed insurgency. However, as Manz goes on to say, the onslaught went far beyond what was militarily necessary to confront the rebels and 'the actions taken violated universally accepted rules of war, let alone the most elemental concepts of human decency'.[99] This was quite simply because the real target was always the people. Any guerrillas caught in the assault were a bonus. Several thousand armed insurgents were not a problem for one of the continent's most ruthless armed forces, which by 1982 had been fighting guerrillas in Guatemala for nearly 20 years. A mobilized, politicized indigenous population was a problem; it raised the very real racist neurosis that lies at the heart of the Guatemalan state.

Look to the past and one sees all the old tactics resurrected, couched in new finery, new rhetoric. The *conquistadores* settled Indians in model villages, formed them into work gangs, incorporated them into armies to fight other Indians in someone else's war. It is hard to avoid the conclusion made over 50 years ago — the more Guatemala changes, the more it stays the same.[100]

Since many of those most affected by the violence were among the most isolated and traditional Indians, it is worth asking if they view the army's present strategy of control and integration in a similar light. Essentially, yes. Most Indians see it as the latest cycle in 450 years of similar treatment and even the least educated can articulate an accurate analysis of the conflict. 'It just doesn't suit them that we improve ourselves', commented one Ixil Indian.

Curiously, it is not the wave of deaths itself that Indian communities have found the hardest to cope with but rather the violent manner of death and social upheaval it causes. Death itself is as inevitable as the natural disasters of earthquakes and volcanic eruptions that have moulded the Indians' surroundings, but violence and murder were almost unknown in the indigenous communities most affected by the war. One Indian civil patroller put the dilemma thus: 'These patrol members are just humble people who never had the chance to make a decision about whether they wanted to get involved in this killing. They just think there must be a different solution, not killing people.'

But the Guatemalan state's abuses of the indigenous population are, of course, much more general. There are at least three levels on which the Indians suffer human rights abuses.

On one level there is the denial of physical and civil rights expressed in murder, torture, kidnapping and enforced relocation. On another level there is the denial of social and economic rights — health, education, legal wages and market prices for products. Being at the bottom of the pile socially and economically, Indians suffer from the denial of these rights particularly acutely, but the phenomenon is by no means confined to the indigenous ethnic group. Ladinos are also murdered and tortured, sick and illiterate.

What Indians do suffer exclusively is abuse of *cultural rights*. In a nation already noted for its use of legal veneers, the right to a different manner of dress, living, language and outlook is not even recognized *de jure* in the constitution, let alone *de facto* in everyday life.

All these rights are of course intimately interlinked. Because the Indian enjoys no cultural recognition, he suffers particularly damning denials of economic and social rights, one of the most obvious examples being forced to carry out any official business in a second language. But vice versa the process is even more significant. Because the indigenous people have no social, economic or civil rights, their culture is under attack. More than anything it has been socio-economic deprivation that has caused the erosion of indigenous society and it is their lack of access to land that demonstrates it best.

In view of this, what does either side of the polarized political spectrum offer?

After four and a half centuries of rule it is reasonable to assume that the current authorities in Guatemala have little to offer the Indian but more of the same: the institutionalized terror of the army and death squads at worst, cultural integration and paternalism at best.

Paternalism and co-option of Indian leadership, though apparently preferable, might be just as detrimental.

'Paternalism is the stablest form of tyranny because it establishes intimate and personal ties of dependence across ethnic or racial ties of cleavage.'[101] On the other hand, co-option of certain Indian 'representatives' with the aim of creating a government-sanctioned indigenous leadership threatens to further split Indian loyalties.

What the left offers Guatemala's indigenous people is less quantifiable. There is no reason to doubt their commitment to securing the Indians' social, economic and civil rights but many anthropologists are sceptical about whether or not Indians could survive as cultural entities under a leftist regime. They cite Arevalo and Arbenz's attempts to integrate the indigenous population by building up a power base in rural areas and they point to the Sandinistas' initial cultural insensitivity towards the Indian peoples of Nicaragua's Atlantic coast. 'Radical and socialist thought does not tolerate ethnicity.'[102]

Indeed, even the EGP, distinguished by its ethnic approach to the revolution, spoke of the indigenous population's 'integration' into 'the new society'.[103] Furthermore, if the organization was less respectful of ethnic customs and traditions from the autumn of 1981, one possible interpretation is that the movement was becoming too ethnic for its leading ideologues as it repeatedly compromised leftist concepts with indigenous practice.

Given that October 1981 saw the start of a major army counter-insurgency campaign, an even more likely explanation is that cultural respect came to be considered something of a luxury in this period. As one anthropologist observed: 'Even well-intentioned commitments to respect cultural differences may give way before the more urgent need for survival of an organized, disciplined fighting force once an escalating cycle of violence begins.'[104]

All this may indicate that while political groupings battle for indigenous hearts and minds, their future is, in fact, all too predictable. Like aboriginal peoples the world over they will be absorbed as the mechanisms that have traditionally protected them from the outside world are eroded, a penchant for such consumer goods as cassette recorders and digital watches proves fatal, and the government becomes aware of them as a potential 'security threat'.

Fortunately, reality in Guatemala is not so simple. Firstly, there is numerical strength. Despite the fact that tens of thousands of Indians have fled Guatemala and that the national census office applies dubious criteria in dubious ways, preliminary figures for the 1981 census put the indigenous population at 38.7% of the total. A truer estimate would probably be over half the population.

Secondly, anthropologist Sol Tax's observation that indigenous peoples do not necessarily disappear culturally when confronted with persistent contact with the 'modern world system' is as true today as it was when first made in Guatemala in the 1930s. Indian towns within minutes of Guatemala City — such as San Lucas, San Juan, San Pedro Sacatepéquez — illustrate the indigenous determination to persist in their traditional ways in the face of what is often regarded as the threat of the outside world. A missionary describes it thus: 'Four hundred and fifty years ago the Crown sent commissioners to get Indians to eat off tables. They still don't.'

Thirdly, Guatemalan indigenous culture is never stagnant, having developed a remarkable adaptability as part of its will to survive. Some of today's lifestyles and dress would not be recognized by ancestors of a mere two or three generations back, yet remain totally Indian. Indeed, Indians have not only repeatedly adapted to the intrusions of the outside world but have manipulated them to secure the benefits they offer to protect their own culture rather than destroy it. One example of this comes from Jorge Echeverria, who, as accountant to President Jorge Ubico in the 1930s, recalled a petition by Indians in Nahualá asking the president to remove the 'corrupting influence' of a Ladino civil governor, military control and post and telegraph officials. When the president refused, the Indian leaders proposed that they send their own most intelligent youth to the city to be trained for the posts, if the government would send them back to the town as officials to replace the Ladinos. (Incidentally, the president agreed).

Given westernization tendencies and traditional indigenous determination not to be assimilated, these two trends seem to be moving in opposite directions, further accentuating today's divisions among Guatemala's Indians. Several observers have noted a cyclical pattern: 'There's a period of heavy westernization, then there's a reaction with traditional aspects coming right back into fashion.' But, whether or not any traditional revival can be anything more than temporary, considering the economic and social odds against the Indian, is doubtful. It seems more relevant to ask exactly what 'Ladinoization' entails.

For some it is exactly that — a conversion to western language, manner, ways and, most importantly, thinking. Some Indians consciously try to pass as Ladino — usually because it is synonymous with socio-economic improvement — others fall into it more gradually as a result of being cut off from their home community and language group. The process, inevitably, tends to be more common in or near towns and cities where there is more economic incentive to pass, more Ladinos to imitate and more racism to avoid, says one development worker. 'It affects young men worst, it's more modern and *macho* to be western.'

But, true to Indian adaptability, there is another trend. Anthropologists have noted in various areas the growth of a middle group somewhere between the two cultures. Many still define these as Indian — the question really revolves around definitions and more accurately, changing definitions. This 'middle group' includes the increasing number of Indian professionals, such as doctors and lawyers, as well as factory workers, merchants and construction workers, and are regarded as at least partially Indians by Ladinos and indigenous people alike.

The key seems to be values. 'If they keep a traditional Indian sense of respect and responsibility they are still essentially Indian', insists one keen observer. These values could be broadened to include a traditional Indian sense of family, indigenous language and emphasis on social relations with other Indians. This in itself accords with the Indian definition of a fellow Indian. It is a person '*sin respeto*' (without respect) or a '*mala gente*' (bad person) who is classified as '*como Ladino*' (like a Ladino), ie non-Indian. Indian social contacts are important but not completely vital. 'That an indigenous person's personal network includes strong links with non-Indians does not cause him to be classified 'como Ladino'.[105]

But, what of those rural Indians who have managed to remain in their highland villages? Change is obviously coming and it is absurd to oppose it when indigenous people themselves are now showing a strong desire for modern education, health and farming methods. The real debate should revolve around what type of change indigenous communities will face and who will control it.

Indians have shown repeatedly that they can benefit from change offered on a voluntary basis, even using such changes to reinforce indigenous society rather than undermine it. But, the kind of enforced change now being imposed in the western highlands is a completely different matter. Cultural sensitive change is possible, probably its best guarantee being the maximum involvement of indigenous people themselves in any development projects. In specific terms, land reform (along with protection of the existing, eroding land base) and bilingual education would probably do most to protect indigenous society. Meaningful land reform would have to involve expropriation of coffee *fincas* in the highland areas where land rightfully belongs to Indians.

Ultimately, the current situation of Indians in Guatemala is laced with ironies.

Firstly, there is the official belief that Indians want to change Guatemalan society ideologically when this is probably not true. 'I know no real Indian who associates with Marxism, ideologically', says one doctor. The Indians' strong sense of independence and small trader interests would indeed appear to be poor socialist material. Said another observer: 'What the Indian is looking for is a place in Guatemalan society, not its overthrow.'

Secondly, there is the irony of the cynical Ladino belief that Indians have nothing to offer Guatemalan society, when all the indications are to the contrary. The Indians' strong sense of community service, respect for others and even business sense could all be used to reinforce Guatemalan society rather than be regarded as 'subversive' to it — *if* the indigenous people were afforded an equal place in it.

Yet the key issue in the 1990s must be whether there will be any significant numbers of indigenous people left in Guatemala far into the twenty-first century. To many this will sound alarmist but to those who have looked closely at what is happening in the country today it is a real fear. The fact that Guatemala's Maya have survived whatever they have been subjected to in the past does not ensure that they will go on remaining a distinct cultural group in the future.

Never in the past have the country's indigenous people been subjected to forces whose sole object is cultural absorption, as they are being today. Scientific annihilation — the result of the Maya becoming merely the latest group of indigenous people worldwide to be considered a security liability by their respective governments — is a new threat; counter-acting this threat from their current weakened socio-economic position in Guatemalan society will almost certainly be the Maya's greatest challenge yet.

CONCLUSION

Guatemala remains a society dominated by the military. Although a civilian government took over in 1986, real power continues to reside with the army, and as this report demonstrates, the killings, detentions, disappearances and torture have continued, albeit on a slightly lower level, and the civilian militias have been consolidated and strengthened, as have the model villages. By incarcerating Indians in model villages and deliberately undermining their traditional structures, the government of Guatemala is attempting to destroy the Mayan culture and way of life.

The fate of the Maya of Guatemala and other indigenous peoples of Central America is not exclusively an internal matter. The scale of human rights violations in the region has long been on the agenda of the UN Commission on Human Rights and other relevant international and inter-regional bodies. Almost 200,000 refugees are resident in neighbouring countries – primarily Mexico – and for many indigenous communities exile has proved almost as traumatic as the massacres and repression which were the cause of their flight.

The Guatemalan government has long been embarrassed by its poor international image; its lobbying of the General Assembly resulted in a downgrading of UN concern in 1987. The 'Special Rapporteur' was replaced by a 'Special Expert' and an 'improvement' in human rights was recorded. It is now clear that whatever 'improvements' have been made they are cosmetic ones only and that killings, both indiscriminate and selective, torture and intimidation continue. The Guatemalan situation should again receive the highest UN priority of a Special Rapporteur and that furthermore all countries with diplomatic representation, trade or aid links with Guatemala, should make forceful representations to the Guatemalan government regarding human rights.

A few thousand refugees have returned to Guatemala under the stimuli of the Esquipulas peace plan but most fear, rightly, to return under present conditions, when their physical safety cannot be guaranteed in army-controlled areas. Clearly unless peace returns to Guatemala there will be no mass return of refugees. Some initiatives have been made in this respect not only by the peace plan put forward by President Arias of Costa Rica in 1986 and the regional peace agreement signed in August 1989, but also, as this report goes to press in October 1989, by the UN Secretary-General's proposal to send a 625-member peace-keeping force to Central America. The force, to be called Onuca, with personnel from Western Europe, Canada and Latin America, would initially be concerned with the situation in Honduras, Nicaragua and El Salvador. An efficient and neutral force could also have a role in policing the internal situation within Guatemala, taking over from the military and civil patrols and easing the transition to a more normal life within the countryside.

The plight of the half a million displaced people within Guatemala, overwhelmingly Mayans, should also be of international concern. As with the refugees they need the possibility to return to their traditional lands and to resume a way of life more in keeping with their community and values. Once again internal peace in the countryside and an end to army-dominated rule seem the only way that such a movement could take place. Once the refugees and displaced people return, they will need material aid and support, at least initially. Here development agencies, both government and non-government, and the churches can play an important role.

As this report demonstrates the Mayans face not only violations of their civil and political rights but deprivation in the social and economic spheres. Little in the socio-economic order has changed in Guatemala since Independence in 1821. On every indicator – health, education, employment – they are the most unprivileged sector of society. Facilities are oriented almost entirely towards the urban areas, most notably Guatemala City, while the highlands are neglected by the government. Thousands of Indians are forced to migrate every year to the coastal plantations where they work in conditions described by the International Labour Organization as 'totally unacceptable'. Much of the coffee, cotton or sugar produced on these plantations makes its way to western nations. Is it too much to ask that western governments, who are members of the ILO, and companies producing and importing such produce, intervene to ensure that acceptable standards of food and accommodation are available and that at least minimum wages are paid?

The economic crisis has hit Guatemala hard and none harder than the indigenous peoples. In 1988 43% of the Guatemalan population were living below the officially defined poverty line and the government's 'Guatemala 2000' economic plan merely aims to return living standards back to 1980 levels. But, as in many other areas of the world, such 're-structuring' is at the cost of the poor; 'unnecessary' price controls, such as those on beans and sugar, were lifted with the result that their costs rose immediately. But the root cause of Indian poverty, unequal land distribution and tiny plots, has not been tackled by the government and the few positive initiatives have come from non-governmental organizations such as the National Association of Peasants for Land. It is important for the international community to recognize and support these initiatives.

Too often the Maya have been seen merely as victims submitting to a superior force. As this report demonstrates this was a prime tactic of Mayan survival, and for centuries despite the physical submission of the Maya, they retained their distinctive culture and way of life. Today this is also under attack. What is encouraging is the beginnings of Mayan leadership, on their own behalf and along with poor Ladinos. Such initiatives must be publicized and supported and the Maya be granted full human and minority rights within Guatemala if peaceful and participative development is to occur.

FOOTNOTES TO PART II

1. Morley, Sylvanus G., *The Ancient Maya*, Stanford University Press (1946).

2. Redfield, Robert, *The Relations between Indians and Ladinos in Agua Escondida, Guatemala*. America Indigena, Vol.XVI (4), October 1956.

3. Pansini, Jude J., *El Pilar: a plantation microcosm of Guatemalan Ethnicity*, Ph.D. Thesis, University of Rochester, Rochester, New York, 1977.

4. Gillen, John, *The Balance of Threat and Security in Meso-america*.

5. Reina, Ruben E., *The Potter and the Farmer*. Expedition Vol.5 (4).

6. Tax, Sol, *World View and Social Relations in Guatemala*. American Anthropologist 43.

7. Bunch, Roland and Roger, *The Highland Maya: Patterns of Life and Clothing in Indian Guatemala*. Josten's Publications, Visalia (1977).

8. Hurtado, Dr. Juan Jose, in *Maya of Guatemala — Life and Dress* by C.L. Pettersen (ed). Ixchel Textile Museum (1976).

9. Stavenhagen, Rodolfo, *Clases, colonialismo y aculturación: ensayo sobre un sistema de relaciones interétnicas en Meso-america*. América Latina Vol. 6(4).

10. Jonas S. and Tobis D., *Guatemala*. The North American Congress on Latin America (NACLA) (1974).

11. Pansini, J. Jude, ibid., *El Pilar*.

12. Adams, Tani Marilena, *San Martin Jilotepeque: Aspects of the Political and Socio-Economic Structure of a Guatemalan Peasant Community*.

13. Guatemala Working Group (GWG), *Guatemala: The Eternal Struggle*, GWG and War on Want (1982).

14. *Cultural Survival Quarterly*, Vol.7, No.1, Spring 1983.

15. Ministerio de Gobernacion, Guatemala. *Constitution de la Republica de Guatemala* (1985).

16. The World Bank, *Guatemala: Economic and Social Position and Prospects*, The World Bank, Washington D.C. (1978).

17. Oxfam America, Unpublished source.

18. Guatemala Health Rights Support Project, *Reading the Vital Signs: Report of the 1988 Health Delegation to Guatemala* (October 1988).

19. Guatemala Health Rights Support Project, *In Hushed Voices: Testimonies of the Guatemalan Health Movement*, Guatemala Health Rights Support Project (1988).

20. *Reading the Vital Signs*, Ibid.

21. Ibid.

22. *In Hushed Voices*, Ibid.

23. Oxfam America, Unpublished source.

24. Inter-Church Committee on Human Rights in Latin America: 1988 Annual Report on the Human Rights Situation in Guatemala, Toronto, Canada (January 1989).

25. Author's interviews, 1989.

26. Agency for International Development, Washington Development Associates, *Tierra y Trabajo en Guatemala, Una Evaluacion*.

27. Davis, Shelton H. and Hodson, Julie, *Witnesses to Political Violence in Guatemala: The Suppression of a Rural Development Movement*, Oxfam America, Boston (1982).

28. *Tierra y Trabajo en Guatemala*, Ibid.

29. Davis, Shelton H. and Hodson, Julie, Ibid.

30. Ibid.

31. NACLA, *Report on the Americas. Garrison Guatemala*. Vol.XVII (I). NACLA (January-February 1983).

32. *Tierra y Trabajo en Guatemala*, Ibid.

33. Melville, Thomas and Marjorie, *Guatemala: The Politics of Land Ownership*, The Free Press, New York (1971).

34. Bunch, Roland and Roger, Ibid.

35. Adams, Richard N., *Crucifixion by Power*, University of Texas Press, Austin (1970).

36. Adams, Ibid.

37. Unpublished essay by Maryknoll Missioner.

38. Painter, James, *Guatemala, False Hope, False Freedom*, Catholic Institute of International Relations and Latin America Bureau, London (1987).

39. NACLA, *Garrison Guatemala*, Ibid.

40. Newbold, Stokes, *Receptivity to communist-fomented agitation in rural Guatemala*. Economic Development and Cultural Change. Vol.5 (4).

41. The World Bank, Ibid.

42. *Cultural Survival*, Ibid.

43. Unpublished essay by Maryknoll Missioner.

44. NACLA, *Report on the Americas*, 'Visions of the Kingdom, the Latin American Church in Conflict'. Vol. XIX (5) (September/October 1985).

45. Simon, Jean-Marie, *Guatemala: Eternal Spring, Eternal Tyranny*. W.W. Norton and Co. (1987).

46. Ibid.

47. Painter, James, Ibid.

48. Ibid.

49. Payeras, Mario, *Los Dias de la Selva*. Editorial *Nuestro Tiempo*, 1981.

50. NACLA, *Garrison Guatemala*, Ibid.

51. Menendez, Rodriguez, Mario, *Por Esto?* Mexico City (August 1981).

52. Davis, Shelton H. and Hodson, Julie, Ibid.

53. Ibid.

54. Concerned Guatemalan Scholars, *Guatemala: Dare to Struggle, Dare to Win*. Concerned Guatemalan Scholars, New York (October 1981).

55. Companero, *Revista internacional de los pobres del ejercito guerrillero de los pobres de Guatemala*. No.4.

56. Girón Lemus, Roberto, from Bulletin of the Asociación de Cañeros, cited in Inforpress, Guatemala City (28 February 1980).

57. Simon, Jean-Marie, Ibid.

58. *Guatemala: A Government Programme of Political Murder*, Amnesty International, London (1981).

59. Davis, Shelton H. and Hodson, Julie, Ibid.

60. McClintock, Michael, *The American Connection*: Volume Two, Zed Books, London (1985).

61. Amnesty International Special Briefing, *Guatemala — Massive extrajudicial executions in rural areas under the Government of General Efraín Rios Montt*. Amnesty International, London (July 1982).

62. *The New York Times*, Raymond Bonner (18 July 1982).

63. Americas Watch, *Human Rights in Guatemala: No neutrals allowed*, New York, 1982.

64. Washington Office on Latin America, *Security and Development Conditions in the Guatemalan Highlands*, Washington (1985)

65. Ibid.

66. New York Times, *Guatemala Can't Take Two Roads*, New York Times (20 July 1982).

67. Chavez, Lydia, *Guatemala Mobilises Over 700,000 Civilians in Local Patrols*. The New York Times (18 November 1983).

68. Wearne, Phillip, *Death and Rios Montt — The Guatemalan Tragedy Grows*. Encuentro, The Mexico City News Political Supplement. No.31 (20 January 1983).

69. Wearne, Phillip, *We Must Get Rid of the Words Indigenous, Indian*. Encuentro, The Mexico City News Political Supplement. No.5 (15 December 1983).

70. Anderson, Ken and Simon, Jean-Marie, 'Permanent Counterinsurgency in Guatemala', *Telos*, A Quarterly of Critical Thought, Number 73, Fall 1987.

71. Guatemala Church in Exile (IGE). *Guatemala: Security, Development and Democracy*, (1989).

[72] Anderson, Ken and Simon, Jean-Marie, Ibid.

[73] Black, George, *Under the Gun*

[74] Ibid.

[75] Simon, Jean-Marie, *Guatemala: Eternal Spring, Eternal Tyranny*. Ibid.

[76] Ibid.

[77] Ibid.

[78] Americas Watch, *Civil Patrols in Guatemala*, New York (1986).

[79] Author's interview, El Quiché, Guatemala (1984).

[80] Simon, Jean-Marie, Ibid.

[81] Ibid.

[82] Painter, James, Ibid.

[83] Ibid.

[84] Nairn, Allan and Simon, Jean-Marie, 'Bureaucracy of Death', *New Republic*, 30 June 1986.

[85] *Guatemala, The Mutual Support Group*, Americas Watch, 1985.

[86] Author's interview, Guatemala City, 1986.

[87] *Report on Guatemala*, 'New Indian Group Opposes Civil Patrols', January-March 1989, Guatemala News and Information Bureau.

[88] Dewart, Tracey and Eckersley, Michel, 'Guatemala's Girón: Good Shepherd or Pied Piper?' NACLA, *Report on the Americas*, March/April 1988.

[89] Burns, Allan F., 'Resettlement in the U.S.: Kanjobal Maya in Indiantown, Florida', *Cultural Survival Quarterly* 12 (4).

[90] Document on the Republic of Guatemala: Diagnosis, Strategy and Project Proposals. Presented to International Conference on Central American Refugees (Cirefca), May 1989.

[91] Author's Interview, Campeche 1989.

[92] Wearne, Phillip, 'Central American Refugees – A long way from home', *Central American Report*, Summer 1989.

[93] Rigoberta Menchú, 'I . . . Rigoberta Menchú.' An Indian Woman in Guatemala', Verso, 1984.

[94] 'U.N. Presentation by Indigenous Groups', *Central America Report*, Inforpress, 26 August 1988.

[95] Simon, Jean-Marie, Ibid.

[96] Asman, David, 'Guatemala in Clearer Focus', *The Wall Street Journal*, 30 April 1984.

[97] Guatemala Church in Exile (IGE).

[98] Manz, Beatriz, *Refugees of a Hidden War*, State University of New York Press, 1988.

[99] Ibid.

[100] Lloyd-Jones, Chester, *Guatemala, Past and Present*, University of Minnesota Press, Minneapolis (1940).

[101] Colby, Benjamin and Van den Berge, Pierre L., *Ixil Country: A plural society in highland Guatemala*, University of California Press, Berkely (1969).

[102] *Cultural Survival Quarterly*, Vol.7, No.1, Ibid.

[103] Companero, Ibid.

[104] *Cultural Survival Quarterly*, Ibid.

[105] Pansini, Jude J., El Pilar, Ibid.

A VERY SELECT BIBLIOGRAPHY

AMERICAS WATCH REPORT, *Human Rights in Guatemala: no neutrals allowed.*

AMERCIAS WATCH REPORT, *Persecuting Human Rights Monitors, The CERJ in Guatemala*, 1989

BLACK, GEORGE, *Guatemala: The Making of a Revolution*, Zed Press, 1984

BLACK, GEORGE, *Garrison Guatemala*, Zed Press, 1984.

COMISION DE DERECHOS HUMANOS DE GUATEMALA, *Preliminary Report submitted to the United Nations of the situation of human rights and basic liberties in Guatemala*, July/October 1983.

CORMACK, M. (Ed.), *Harvest of Violence: the Mayan Indians and the Guatemala Crisis*, University of Oklahoma Press, 1988.

FRIED, J.L., *Guatemala in rebellion: unfinished history*, Grove Press, 1983.

THE GLOBAL REPORT, *The Case for Political Asylum: Guatemala's Uprooted Indians*, RAI, Vol. 1, No. 3.

HARDY, JIM, *Gift of the Devil: a History of Guatemala*, Between the Lines Press, Canada, 1984.

INTERNATIONAL HUMAN RIGHTS LAW GROUP, *Maximizing Deniability: The Justice System and Human Rights in Guatemala*, prepared by Kenneth Anderson, Washington, 1989

McCLINTOCK, M., *Guatemala: The American Connection, State Terror and Popular Resistance*, Zed Press, 1984.

MANZ, BEATRIX, *Refugees of a Hidden War*, State University of New York Press, 1988.

MENCHÚ, RIGOBERTA, edited by Burges Debray, Elisabeth, *'I . . . Rigoberta Menchú.' An Indian Woman in Guatemala*, Verso, 1984.

NASH, *Machine Age Maya: Industrialization of a Guatemalan Community*, University of Chicago Press, 1968.

NELSON, C. and TAYLOR, K., *Witness to Genocide – the present situation of Indians in Guatemala*, Survival International, 1983.

PAINTER, JAMES, *False Hope, False Freedom*, Catholic Institute of International Relations and Latin America Bureau, London, 1987.

PLANT, R., *Unnatural Disaster*, Latin American Bureau, 1978.

SIMON, JEAN MARIE, *Guatemala, Eternal Spring, Eternal Tyranny*, W.W. Norton and Co, New York and London, 1987.

STELTZER, *Health in the Highlands of Guatemala*, University of Washington Press, 1983.

WRIGHT, ROLAND, *Time among the Maya*, Bodley Head, London, 1989.